C-2257   CAREER EXAMINATION SERIES

This is your
PASSBOOK for...

Hoisting Machine Operator

Test Preparation Study Guide
Questions & Answers

COPYRIGHT NOTICE

This book is SOLELY intended for, is sold ONLY to, and its use is RESTRICTED to individual, bona fide applicants or candidates who qualify by virtue of having seriously filed applications for appropriate license, certificate, professional and/or promotional advancement, higher school matriculation, scholarship, or other legitimate requirements of education and/or governmental authorities.

This book is NOT intended for use, class instruction, tutoring, training, duplication, copying, reprinting, excerption, or adaptation, etc., by:

1) Other publishers
2) Proprietors and/or Instructors of "Coaching" and/or Preparatory Courses
3) Personnel and/or Training Divisions of commercial, industrial, and governmental organizations
4) Schools, colleges, or universities and/or their departments and staffs, including teachers and other personnel
5) Testing Agencies or Bureaus
6) Study groups which seek by the purchase of a single volume to copy and/or duplicate and/or adapt this material for use by the group as a whole without having purchased individual volumes for each of the members of the group
7) Et al.

Such persons would be in violation of appropriate Federal and State statutes.

PROVISION OF LICENSING AGREEMENTS – Recognized educational, commercial, industrial, and governmental institutions and organizations, and others legitimately engaged in educational pursuits, including training, testing, and measurement activities, may address request for a licensing agreement to the copyright owners, who will determine whether, and under what conditions, including fees and charges, the materials in this book may be used them. In other words, a licensing facility exists for the legitimate use of the material in this book on other than an individual basis. However, it is asseverated and affirmed here that the material in this book CANNOT be used without the receipt of the express permission of such a licensing agreement from the Publishers. Inquiries re licensing should be addressed to the company, attention rights and permissions department.

All rights reserved, including the right of reproduction in whole or in part, in any form or by any means, electronic or mechanical, including photocopying, recording, or by any information storage and retrieval system, without permission in writing from the Publisher.

Copyright © 2024 by
National Learning Corporation

212 Michael Drive, Syosset, NY 11791
(516) 921-8888 • www.passbooks.com
E-mail: info@passbooks.com

PUBLISHED IN THE UNITED STATES OF AMERICA

PASSBOOK® SERIES

THE *PASSBOOK® SERIES* has been created to prepare applicants and candidates for the ultimate academic battlefield – the examination room.

At some time in our lives, each and every one of us may be required to take an examination – for validation, matriculation, admission, qualification, registration, certification, or licensure.

Based on the assumption that every applicant or candidate has met the basic formal educational standards, has taken the required number of courses, and read the necessary texts, the *PASSBOOK® SERIES* furnishes the one special preparation which may assure passing with confidence, instead of failing with insecurity. Examination questions – together with answers – are furnished as the basic vehicle for study so that the mysteries of the examination and its compounding difficulties may be eliminated or diminished by a sure method.

This book is meant to help you pass your examination provided that you qualify and are serious in your objective.

The entire field is reviewed through the huge store of content information which is succinctly presented through a provocative and challenging approach – the question-and-answer method.

A climate of success is established by furnishing the correct answers at the end of each test.

You soon learn to recognize types of questions, forms of questions, and patterns of questioning. You may even begin to anticipate expected outcomes.

You perceive that many questions are repeated or adapted so that you can gain acute insights, which may enable you to score many sure points.

You learn how to confront new questions, or types of questions, and to attack them confidently and work out the correct answers.

You note objectives and emphases, and recognize pitfalls and dangers, so that you may make positive educational adjustments.

Moreover, you are kept fully informed in relation to new concepts, methods, practices, and directions in the field.

You discover that you are actually taking the examination all the time: you are preparing for the examination by "taking" an examination, not by reading extraneous and/or supererogatory textbooks.

In short, this PASSBOOK®, used directedly, should be an important factor in helping you to pass your test.

HOISTING MACHINE OPERATOR

CLASSIFICATION OF LICENSES
1. Basic License: The Basic License is required to operate cranes, derricks and cableways, excluding power-operated cranes with booms, including jibs and other extensions, which exceed two hundred feet in length and truck-mounted tower cranes which exceed two hundred feet in height.
2. Endorsement on Basic License: This Endorsement will permit persons who possess a Basic License to operate hoisting machinery without limitation or restriction.

REQUIREMENTS
Applicants must meet the following qualifications at the time of filing for this examination:
1. Be at least 21 years of age;
2. Be able to read and write the English language;
3. Applicants for the Basic License shall have had at least 2 years' prior experience as an oiler or as an assistant to an operator on cranes, derricks or cableways.
4. Applicants for the Endorsement on Basic License must possess a valid Basic License and shall have had at least 2 years of experience as an assistant to an operator on cranes with booms, including jibs and other extensions exceeding two hundred feet in length or truck-mounted tower cranes exceeding two hundred feet in height.

SCOPE OF EXAMINATION
The examination for the Basic License will consist of a written test of the multiple-choice type and a practical-oral test. The written test is to determine the candidate's knowledge of the operation, safety and repair of: internal combustion engines, electric motors; motor controllers; motor-generator sets; transmissions; clutches; brakes; hoisting drums; wire rope; and related subjects. The practical-oral test will be given to those candidates who pass the written test. The practical-oral test will be held on construction equipment and will test the candidate's knowledge of actual operation, adjustment, maintenance and repair of portable construction equipment driven by motive power other than steam. The examination for the Endorsement will consist of a practical-oral test only. Candidates will be required to have the Basic License in order to apply for the test for the Endorsement. Candidates must receive at least 70 percent in the written test and 70 percent in the practical-oral test to qualify for the Basic License and the Endorsement. Examinations will be held from time to time as conditions warrant.

HOW TO TAKE A TEST

I. YOU MUST PASS AN EXAMINATION

A. WHAT EVERY CANDIDATE SHOULD KNOW

Examination applicants often ask us for help in preparing for the written test. What can I study in advance? What kinds of questions will be asked? How will the test be given? How will the papers be graded?

As an applicant for a civil service examination, you may be wondering about some of these things. Our purpose here is to suggest effective methods of advance study and to describe civil service examinations.

Your chances for success on this examination can be increased if you know how to prepare. Those "pre-examination jitters" can be reduced if you know what to expect. You can even experience an adventure in good citizenship if you know why civil service exams are given.

B. WHY ARE CIVIL SERVICE EXAMINATIONS GIVEN?

Civil service examinations are important to you in two ways. As a citizen, you want public jobs filled by employees who know how to do their work. As a job seeker, you want a fair chance to compete for that job on an equal footing with other candidates. The best-known means of accomplishing this two-fold goal is the competitive examination.

Exams are widely publicized throughout the nation. They may be administered for jobs in federal, state, city, municipal, town or village governments or agencies.

Any citizen may apply, with some limitations, such as the age or residence of applicants. Your experience and education may be reviewed to see whether you meet the requirements for the particular examination. When these requirements exist, they are reasonable and applied consistently to all applicants. Thus, a competitive examination may cause you some uneasiness now, but it is your privilege and safeguard.

C. HOW ARE CIVIL SERVICE EXAMS DEVELOPED?

Examinations are carefully written by trained technicians who are specialists in the field known as "psychological measurement," in consultation with recognized authorities in the field of work that the test will cover. These experts recommend the subject matter areas or skills to be tested; only those knowledges or skills important to your success on the job are included. The most reliable books and source materials available are used as references. Together, the experts and technicians judge the difficulty level of the questions.

Test technicians know how to phrase questions so that the problem is clearly stated. Their ethics do not permit "trick" or "catch" questions. Questions may have been tried out on sample groups, or subjected to statistical analysis, to determine their usefulness.

Written tests are often used in combination with performance tests, ratings of training and experience, and oral interviews. All of these measures combine to form the best-known means of finding the right person for the right job.

II. HOW TO PASS THE WRITTEN TEST

A. NATURE OF THE EXAMINATION

To prepare intelligently for civil service examinations, you should know how they differ from school examinations you have taken. In school you were assigned certain definite pages to read or subjects to cover. The examination questions were quite detailed and usually emphasized memory. Civil service exams, on the other hand, try to discover your present ability to perform the duties of a position, plus your potentiality to learn these duties. In other words, a civil service exam attempts to predict how successful you will be. Questions cover such a broad area that they cannot be as minute and detailed as school exam questions.

In the public service similar kinds of work, or positions, are grouped together in one "class." This process is known as *position-classification*. All the positions in a class are paid according to the salary range for that class. One class title covers all of these positions, and they are all tested by the same examination.

B. FOUR BASIC STEPS

1) Study the announcement

How, then, can you know what subjects to study? Our best answer is: "Learn as much as possible about the class of positions for which you've applied." The exam will test the knowledge, skills and abilities needed to do the work.

Your most valuable source of information about the position you want is the official exam announcement. This announcement lists the training and experience qualifications. Check these standards and apply only if you come reasonably close to meeting them.

The brief description of the position in the examination announcement offers some clues to the subjects which will be tested. Think about the job itself. Review the duties in your mind. Can you perform them, or are there some in which you are rusty? Fill in the blank spots in your preparation.

Many jurisdictions preview the written test in the exam announcement by including a section called "Knowledge and Abilities Required," "Scope of the Examination," or some similar heading. Here you will find out specifically what fields will be tested.

2) Review your own background

Once you learn in general what the position is all about, and what you need to know to do the work, ask yourself which subjects you already know fairly well and which need improvement. You may wonder whether to concentrate on improving your strong areas or on building some background in your fields of weakness. When the announcement has specified "some knowledge" or "considerable knowledge," or has used adjectives like "beginning principles of..." or "advanced ... methods," you can get a clue as to the number and difficulty of questions to be asked in any given field. More questions, and hence broader coverage, would be included for those subjects which are more important in the work. Now weigh your strengths and weaknesses against the job requirements and prepare accordingly.

3) Determine the level of the position

Another way to tell how intensively you should prepare is to understand the level of the job for which you are applying. Is it the entering level? In other words, is this the position in which beginners in a field of work are hired? Or is it an intermediate or advanced level? Sometimes this is indicated by such words as "Junior" or "Senior" in the class title. Other jurisdictions use Roman numerals to designate the level – Clerk I, Clerk II, for example. The word "Supervisor" sometimes appears in the title. If the level is not indicated by the title, check the description of duties. Will you be working under very close supervision, or will you have responsibility for independent decisions in this work?

4) Choose appropriate study materials

Now that you know the subjects to be examined and the relative amount of each subject to be covered, you can choose suitable study materials. For beginning level jobs, or even advanced ones, if you have a pronounced weakness in some aspect of your training, read a modern, standard textbook in that field. Be sure it is up to date and has general coverage. Such books are normally available at your library, and the librarian will be glad to help you locate one. For entry-level positions, questions of appropriate difficulty are chosen – neither highly advanced questions, nor those too simple. Such questions require careful thought but not advanced training.

If the position for which you are applying is technical or advanced, you will read more advanced, specialized material. If you are already familiar with the basic principles of your field, elementary textbooks would waste your time. Concentrate on advanced textbooks and technical periodicals. Think through the concepts and review difficult problems in your field.

These are all general sources. You can get more ideas on your own initiative, following these leads. For example, training manuals and publications of the government agency which employs workers in your field can be useful, particularly for technical and professional positions. A letter or visit to the government department involved may result in more specific study suggestions, and certainly will provide you with a more definite idea of the exact nature of the position you are seeking.

III. KINDS OF TESTS

Tests are used for purposes other than measuring knowledge and ability to perform specified duties. For some positions, it is equally important to test ability to make adjustments to new situations or to profit from training. In others, basic mental abilities not dependent on information are essential. Questions which test these things may not appear as pertinent to the duties of the position as those which test for knowledge and information. Yet they are often highly important parts of a fair examination. For very general questions, it is almost impossible to help you direct your study efforts. What we can do is to point out some of the more common of these general abilities needed in public service positions and describe some typical questions.

1) General information

Broad, general information has been found useful for predicting job success in some kinds of work. This is tested in a variety of ways, from vocabulary lists to questions about current events. Basic background in some field of work, such as sociology or economics, may be sampled in a group of questions. Often these are principles which have become familiar to most persons through exposure rather than through formal training. It is difficult to advise you how to study for these questions; being alert to the world around you is our best suggestion.

2) Verbal ability

An example of an ability needed in many positions is verbal or language ability. Verbal ability is, in brief, the ability to use and understand words. Vocabulary and grammar tests are typical measures of this ability. Reading comprehension or paragraph interpretation questions are common in many kinds of civil service tests. You are given a paragraph of written material and asked to find its central meaning.

3) Numerical ability

Number skills can be tested by the familiar arithmetic problem, by checking paired lists of numbers to see which are alike and which are different, or by interpreting charts and graphs. In the latter test, a graph may be printed in the test booklet which you are asked to use as the basis for answering questions.

4) Observation

A popular test for law-enforcement positions is the observation test. A picture is shown to you for several minutes, then taken away. Questions about the picture test your ability to observe both details and larger elements.

5) Following directions

In many positions in the public service, the employee must be able to carry out written instructions dependably and accurately. You may be given a chart with several columns, each column listing a variety of information. The questions require you to carry out directions involving the information given in the chart.

6) Skills and aptitudes

Performance tests effectively measure some manual skills and aptitudes. When the skill is one in which you are trained, such as typing or shorthand, you can practice. These tests are often very much like those given in business school or high school courses. For many of the other skills and aptitudes, however, no short-time preparation can be made. Skills and abilities natural to you or that you have developed throughout your lifetime are being tested.

Many of the general questions just described provide all the data needed to answer the questions and ask you to use your reasoning ability to find the answers. Your best preparation for these tests, as well as for tests of facts and ideas, is to be at your physical and mental best. You, no doubt, have your own methods of getting into an exam-taking mood and keeping "in shape." The next section lists some ideas on this subject.

IV. KINDS OF QUESTIONS

Only rarely is the "essay" question, which you answer in narrative form, used in civil service tests. Civil service tests are usually of the short-answer type. Full instructions for answering these questions will be given to you at the examination. But in case this is your first experience with short-answer questions and separate answer sheets, here is what you need to know:

1) **Multiple-choice Questions**

Most popular of the short-answer questions is the "multiple choice" or "best answer" question. It can be used, for example, to test for factual knowledge, ability to solve problems or judgment in meeting situations found at work.

A multiple-choice question is normally one of three types—
- It can begin with an incomplete statement followed by several possible endings. You are to find the one ending which *best* completes the statement, although some of the others may not be entirely wrong.
- It can also be a complete statement in the form of a question which is answered by choosing one of the statements listed.

- It can be in the form of a problem – again you select the best answer.

Here is an example of a multiple-choice question with a discussion which should give you some clues as to the method for choosing the right answer:

When an employee has a complaint about his assignment, the action which will *best* help him overcome his difficulty is to
- A. discuss his difficulty with his coworkers
- B. take the problem to the head of the organization
- C. take the problem to the person who gave him the assignment
- D. say nothing to anyone about his complaint

In answering this question, you should study each of the choices to find which is best. Consider choice "A" – Certainly an employee may discuss his complaint with fellow employees, but no change or improvement can result, and the complaint remains unresolved. Choice "B" is a poor choice since the head of the organization probably does not know what assignment you have been given, and taking your problem to him is known as "going over the head" of the supervisor. The supervisor, or person who made the assignment, is the person who can clarify it or correct any injustice. Choice "C" is, therefore, correct. To say nothing, as in choice "D," is unwise. Supervisors have and interest in knowing the problems employees are facing, and the employee is seeking a solution to his problem.

2) True/False Questions

The "true/false" or "right/wrong" form of question is sometimes used. Here a complete statement is given. Your job is to decide whether the statement is right or wrong.

SAMPLE: A roaming cell-phone call to a nearby city costs less than a non-roaming call to a distant city.

This statement is wrong, or false, since roaming calls are more expensive.

This is not a complete list of all possible question forms, although most of the others are variations of these common types. You will always get complete directions for answering questions. Be sure you understand *how* to mark your answers – ask questions until you do.

V. RECORDING YOUR ANSWERS

Computer terminals are used more and more today for many different kinds of exams.

For an examination with very few applicants, you may be told to record your answers in the test booklet itself. Separate answer sheets are much more common. If this separate answer sheet is to be scored by machine – and this is often the case – it is highly important that you mark your answers correctly in order to get credit.

An electronic scoring machine is often used in civil service offices because of the speed with which papers can be scored. Machine-scored answer sheets must be marked with a pencil, which will be given to you. This pencil has a high graphite content which responds to the electronic scoring machine. As a matter of fact, stray dots may register as answers, so do not let your pencil rest on the answer sheet while you are pondering the correct answer. Also, if your pencil lead breaks or is otherwise defective, ask for another.

Since the answer sheet will be dropped in a slot in the scoring machine, be careful not to bend the corners or get the paper crumpled.

The answer sheet normally has five vertical columns of numbers, with 30 numbers to a column. These numbers correspond to the question numbers in your test booklet. After each number, going across the page are four or five pairs of dotted lines. These short dotted lines have small letters or numbers above them. The first two pairs may also have a "T" or "F" above the letters. This indicates that the first two pairs only are to be used if the questions are of the true-false type. If the questions are multiple choice, disregard the "T" and "F" and pay attention only to the small letters or numbers.

Answer your questions in the manner of the sample that follows:

32. The largest city in the United States is
    A. Washington, D.C.
    B. New York City
    C. Chicago
    D. Detroit
    E. San Francisco

1) Choose the answer you think is best. (New York City is the largest, so "B" is correct.)
2) Find the row of dotted lines numbered the same as the question you are answering. (Find row number 32)
3) Find the pair of dotted lines corresponding to the answer. (Find the pair of lines under the mark "B.")
4) Make a solid black mark between the dotted lines.

VI. BEFORE THE TEST

Common sense will help you find procedures to follow to get ready for an examination. Too many of us, however, overlook these sensible measures. Indeed, nervousness and fatigue have been found to be the most serious reasons why applicants fail to do their best on civil service tests. Here is a list of reminders:

- Begin your preparation early – Don't wait until the last minute to go scurrying around for books and materials or to find out what the position is all about.
- Prepare continuously – An hour a night for a week is better than an all-night cram session. This has been definitely established. What is more, a night a week for a month will return better dividends than crowding your study into a shorter period of time.
- Locate the place of the exam – You have been sent a notice telling you when and where to report for the examination. If the location is in a different town or otherwise unfamiliar to you, it would be well to inquire the best route and learn something about the building.
- Relax the night before the test – Allow your mind to rest. Do not study at all that night. Plan some mild recreation or diversion; then go to bed early and get a good night's sleep.
- Get up early enough to make a leisurely trip to the place for the test – This way unforeseen events, traffic snarls, unfamiliar buildings, etc. will not upset you.
- Dress comfortably – A written test is not a fashion show. You will be known by number and not by name, so wear something comfortable.

- Leave excess paraphernalia at home – Shopping bags and odd bundles will get in your way. You need bring only the items mentioned in the official notice you received; usually everything you need is provided. Do not bring reference books to the exam. They will only confuse those last minutes and be taken away from you when in the test room.
- Arrive somewhat ahead of time – If because of transportation schedules you must get there very early, bring a newspaper or magazine to take your mind off yourself while waiting.
- Locate the examination room – When you have found the proper room, you will be directed to the seat or part of the room where you will sit. Sometimes you are given a sheet of instructions to read while you are waiting. Do not fill out any forms until you are told to do so; just read them and be prepared.
- Relax and prepare to listen to the instructions
- If you have any physical problem that may keep you from doing your best, be sure to tell the test administrator. If you are sick or in poor health, you really cannot do your best on the exam. You can come back and take the test some other time.

VII. AT THE TEST

The day of the test is here and you have the test booklet in your hand. The temptation to get going is very strong. Caution! There is more to success than knowing the right answers. You must know how to identify your papers and understand variations in the type of short-answer question used in this particular examination. Follow these suggestions for maximum results from your efforts:

1) Cooperate with the monitor

The test administrator has a duty to create a situation in which you can be as much at ease as possible. He will give instructions, tell you when to begin, check to see that you are marking your answer sheet correctly, and so on. He is not there to guard you, although he will see that your competitors do not take unfair advantage. He wants to help you do your best.

2) Listen to all instructions

Don't jump the gun! Wait until you understand all directions. In most civil service tests you get more time than you need to answer the questions. So don't be in a hurry. Read each word of instructions until you clearly understand the meaning. Study the examples, listen to all announcements and follow directions. Ask questions if you do not understand what to do.

3) Identify your papers

Civil service exams are usually identified by number only. You will be assigned a number; you must not put your name on your test papers. Be sure to copy your number correctly. Since more than one exam may be given, copy your exact examination title.

4) Plan your time

Unless you are told that a test is a "speed" or "rate of work" test, speed itself is usually not important. Time enough to answer all the questions will be provided, but this does not mean that you have all day. An overall time limit has been set. Divide the total time (in minutes) by the number of questions to determine the approximate time you have for each question.

5) Do not linger over difficult questions

If you come across a difficult question, mark it with a paper clip (useful to have along) and come back to it when you have been through the booklet. One caution if you do this – be sure to skip a number on your answer sheet as well. Check often to be sure that you have not lost your place and that you are marking in the row numbered the same as the question you are answering.

6) Read the questions

Be sure you know what the question asks! Many capable people are unsuccessful because they failed to *read* the questions correctly.

7) Answer all questions

Unless you have been instructed that a penalty will be deducted for incorrect answers, it is better to guess than to omit a question.

8) Speed tests

It is often better NOT to guess on speed tests. It has been found that on timed tests people are tempted to spend the last few seconds before time is called in marking answers at random – without even reading them – in the hope of picking up a few extra points. To discourage this practice, the instructions may warn you that your score will be "corrected" for guessing. That is, a penalty will be applied. The incorrect answers will be deducted from the correct ones, or some other penalty formula will be used.

9) Review your answers

If you finish before time is called, go back to the questions you guessed or omitted to give them further thought. Review other answers if you have time.

10) Return your test materials

If you are ready to leave before others have finished or time is called, take ALL your materials to the monitor and leave quietly. Never take any test material with you. The monitor can discover whose papers are not complete, and taking a test booklet may be grounds for disqualification.

VIII. EXAMINATION TECHNIQUES

1) Read the general instructions carefully. These are usually printed on the first page of the exam booklet. As a rule, these instructions refer to the timing of the examination; the fact that you should not start work until the signal and must stop work at a signal, etc. If there are any *special* instructions, such as a choice of questions to be answered, make sure that you note this instruction carefully.

2) When you are ready to start work on the examination, that is as soon as the signal has been given, read the instructions to each question booklet, underline any key words or phrases, such as *least, best, outline, describe* and the like. In this way you will tend to answer as requested rather than discover on reviewing your paper that you *listed without describing*, that you selected the *worst* choice rather than the *best* choice, etc.

3) If the examination is of the objective or multiple-choice type – that is, each question will also give a series of possible answers: A, B, C or D, and you are called upon to select the best answer and write the letter next to that answer on your answer paper – it is advisable to start answering each question in turn. There may be anywhere from 50 to 100 such questions in the three or four hours allotted and you can see how much time would be taken if you read through all the questions before beginning to answer any. Furthermore, if you come across a question or group of questions which you know would be difficult to answer, it would undoubtedly affect your handling of all the other questions.

4) If the examination is of the essay type and contains but a few questions, it is a moot point as to whether you should read all the questions before starting to answer any one. Of course, if you are given a choice – say five out of seven and the like – then it is essential to read all the questions so you can eliminate the two that are most difficult. If, however, you are asked to answer all the questions, there may be danger in trying to answer the easiest one first because you may find that you will spend too much time on it. The best technique is to answer the first question, then proceed to the second, etc.

5) Time your answers. Before the exam begins, write down the time it started, then add the time allowed for the examination and write down the time it must be completed, then divide the time available somewhat as follows:
   - If 3-1/2 hours are allowed, that would be 210 minutes. If you have 80 objective-type questions, that would be an average of 2-1/2 minutes per question. Allow yourself no more than 2 minutes per question, or a total of 160 minutes, which will permit about 50 minutes to review.
   - If for the time allotment of 210 minutes there are 7 essay questions to answer, that would average about 30 minutes a question. Give yourself only 25 minutes per question so that you have about 35 minutes to review.

6) The most important instruction is to *read each question* and make sure you know what is wanted. The second most important instruction is to *time yourself properly* so that you answer every question. The third most important instruction is to *answer every question*. Guess if you have to but include something for each question. Remember that you will receive no credit for a blank and will probably receive some credit if you write something in answer to an essay question. If you guess a letter – say "B" for a multiple-choice question – you may have guessed right. If you leave a blank as an answer to a multiple-choice question, the examiners may respect your feelings but it will not add a point to your score. Some exams may penalize you for wrong answers, so in such cases *only*, you may not want to guess unless you have some basis for your answer.

7) Suggestions
   a. Objective-type questions
      1. Examine the question booklet for proper sequence of pages and questions
      2. Read all instructions carefully
      3. Skip any question which seems too difficult; return to it after all other questions have been answered
      4. Apportion your time properly; do not spend too much time on any single question or group of questions

5. Note and underline key words – *all, most, fewest, least, best, worst, same, opposite,* etc.
6. Pay particular attention to negatives
7. Note unusual option, e.g., unduly long, short, complex, different or similar in content to the body of the question
8. Observe the use of "hedging" words – *probably, may, most likely,* etc.
9. Make sure that your answer is put next to the same number as the question
10. Do not second-guess unless you have good reason to believe the second answer is definitely more correct
11. Cross out original answer if you decide another answer is more accurate; do not erase until you are ready to hand your paper in
12. Answer all questions; guess unless instructed otherwise
13. Leave time for review

   b. Essay questions
      1. Read each question carefully
      2. Determine exactly what is wanted. Underline key words or phrases.
      3. Decide on outline or paragraph answer
      4. Include many different points and elements unless asked to develop any one or two points or elements
      5. Show impartiality by giving pros and cons unless directed to select one side only
      6. Make and write down any assumptions you find necessary to answer the questions
      7. Watch your English, grammar, punctuation and choice of words
      8. Time your answers; don't crowd material

8) Answering the essay question

Most essay questions can be answered by framing the specific response around several key words or ideas. Here are a few such key words or ideas:

M's: manpower, materials, methods, money, management
P's: purpose, program, policy, plan, procedure, practice, problems, pitfalls, personnel, public relations

   a. Six basic steps in handling problems:
      1. Preliminary plan and background development
      2. Collect information, data and facts
      3. Analyze and interpret information, data and facts
      4. Analyze and develop solutions as well as make recommendations
      5. Prepare report and sell recommendations
      6. Install recommendations and follow up effectiveness

   b. Pitfalls to avoid
      1. *Taking things for granted* – A statement of the situation does not necessarily imply that each of the elements is necessarily true; for example, a complaint may be invalid and biased so that all that can be taken for granted is that a complaint has been registered

2. *Considering only one side of a situation* – Wherever possible, indicate several alternatives and then point out the reasons you selected the best one
3. *Failing to indicate follow up* – Whenever your answer indicates action on your part, make certain that you will take proper follow-up action to see how successful your recommendations, procedures or actions turn out to be
4. *Taking too long in answering any single question* – Remember to time your answers properly

IX. AFTER THE TEST

Scoring procedures differ in detail among civil service jurisdictions although the general principles are the same. Whether the papers are hand-scored or graded by machine we have described, they are nearly always graded by number. That is, the person who marks the paper knows only the number – never the name – of the applicant. Not until all the papers have been graded will they be matched with names. If other tests, such as training and experience or oral interview ratings have been given, scores will be combined. Different parts of the examination usually have different weights. For example, the written test might count 60 percent of the final grade, and a rating of training and experience 40 percent. In many jurisdictions, veterans will have a certain number of points added to their grades.

After the final grade has been determined, the names are placed in grade order and an eligible list is established. There are various methods for resolving ties between those who get the same final grade – probably the most common is to place first the name of the person whose application was received first. Job offers are made from the eligible list in the order the names appear on it. You will be notified of your grade and your rank as soon as all these computations have been made. This will be done as rapidly as possible.

People who are found to meet the requirements in the announcement are called "eligibles." Their names are put on a list of eligible candidates. An eligible's chances of getting a job depend on how high he stands on this list and how fast agencies are filling jobs from the list.

When a job is to be filled from a list of eligibles, the agency asks for the names of people on the list of eligibles for that job. When the civil service commission receives this request, it sends to the agency the names of the three people highest on this list. Or, if the job to be filled has specialized requirements, the office sends the agency the names of the top three persons who meet these requirements from the general list.

The appointing officer makes a choice from among the three people whose names were sent to him. If the selected person accepts the appointment, the names of the others are put back on the list to be considered for future openings.

That is the rule in hiring from all kinds of eligible lists, whether they are for typist, carpenter, chemist, or something else. For every vacancy, the appointing officer has his choice of any one of the top three eligibles on the list. This explains why the person whose name is on top of the list sometimes does not get an appointment when some of the persons lower on the list do. If the appointing officer chooses the second or third eligible, the No. 1 eligible does not get a job at once, but stays on the list until he is appointed or the list is terminated.

X. HOW TO PASS THE INTERVIEW TEST

The examination for which you applied requires an oral interview test. You have already taken the written test and you are now being called for the interview test – the final part of the formal examination.

You may think that it is not possible to prepare for an interview test and that there are no procedures to follow during an interview. Our purpose is to point out some things you can do in advance that will help you and some good rules to follow and pitfalls to avoid while you are being interviewed.

What is an interview supposed to test?

The written examination is designed to test the technical knowledge and competence of the candidate; the oral is designed to evaluate intangible qualities, not readily measured otherwise, and to establish a list showing the relative fitness of each candidate – as measured against his competitors – for the position sought. Scoring is not on the basis of "right" and "wrong," but on a sliding scale of values ranging from "not passable" to "outstanding." As a matter of fact, it is possible to achieve a relatively low score without a single "incorrect" answer because of evident weakness in the qualities being measured.

Occasionally, an examination may consist entirely of an oral test – either an individual or a group oral. In such cases, information is sought concerning the technical knowledges and abilities of the candidate, since there has been no written examination for this purpose. More commonly, however, an oral test is used to supplement a written examination.

Who conducts interviews?

The composition of oral boards varies among different jurisdictions. In nearly all, a representative of the personnel department serves as chairman. One of the members of the board may be a representative of the department in which the candidate would work. In some cases, "outside experts" are used, and, frequently, a businessman or some other representative of the general public is asked to serve. Labor and management or other special groups may be represented. The aim is to secure the services of experts in the appropriate field.

However the board is composed, it is a good idea (and not at all improper or unethical) to ascertain in advance of the interview who the members are and what groups they represent. When you are introduced to them, you will have some idea of their backgrounds and interests, and at least you will not stutter and stammer over their names.

What should be done before the interview?

While knowledge about the board members is useful and takes some of the surprise element out of the interview, there is other preparation which is more substantive. It *is* possible to prepare for an oral interview – in several ways:

1) Keep a copy of your application and review it carefully before the interview

This may be the only document before the oral board, and the starting point of the interview. Know what education and experience you have listed there, and the sequence and dates of all of it. Sometimes the board will ask you to review the highlights of your experience for them; you should not have to hem and haw doing it.

2) Study the class specification and the examination announcement

Usually, the oral board has one or both of these to guide them. The qualities, characteristics or knowledges required by the position sought are stated in these documents. They offer valuable clues as to the nature of the oral interview. For example, if the job involves supervisory responsibilities, the announcement will usually indicate that knowledge of modern supervisory methods and the qualifications of the candidate as a supervisor will be tested. If so, you can expect such questions, frequently in the form of a hypothetical situation which you are expected to solve. NEVER go into an oral without knowledge of the duties and responsibilities of the job you seek.

3) Think through each qualification required

Try to visualize the kind of questions you would ask if you were a board member. How well could you answer them? Try especially to appraise your own knowledge and background in each area, *measured against the job sought*, and identify any areas in which you are weak. Be critical and realistic – do not flatter yourself.

4) Do some general reading in areas in which you feel you may be weak

For example, if the job involves supervision and your past experience has NOT, some general reading in supervisory methods and practices, particularly in the field of human relations, might be useful. Do NOT study agency procedures or detailed manuals. The oral board will be testing your understanding and capacity, not your memory.

5) Get a good night's sleep and watch your general health and mental attitude

You will want a clear head at the interview. Take care of a cold or any other minor ailment, and of course, no hangovers.

What should be done on the day of the interview?

Now comes the day of the interview itself. Give yourself plenty of time to get there. Plan to arrive somewhat ahead of the scheduled time, particularly if your appointment is in the fore part of the day. If a previous candidate fails to appear, the board might be ready for you a bit early. By early afternoon an oral board is almost invariably behind schedule if there are many candidates, and you may have to wait. Take along a book or magazine to read, or your application to review, but leave any extraneous material in the waiting room when you go in for your interview. In any event, relax and compose yourself.

The matter of dress is important. The board is forming impressions about you – from your experience, your manners, your attitude, and your appearance. Give your personal appearance careful attention. Dress your best, but not your flashiest. Choose conservative, appropriate clothing, and be sure it is immaculate. This is a business interview, and your appearance should indicate that you regard it as such. Besides, being well groomed and properly dressed will help boost your confidence.

Sooner or later, someone will call your name and escort you into the interview room. *This is it.* From here on you are on your own. It is too late for any more preparation. But remember, you asked for this opportunity to prove your fitness, and you are here because your request was granted.

What happens when you go in?

The usual sequence of events will be as follows: The clerk (who is often the board stenographer) will introduce you to the chairman of the oral board, who will introduce you to the other members of the board. Acknowledge the introductions before you sit down. Do not be surprised if you find a microphone facing you or a stenotypist sitting by. Oral interviews are usually recorded in the event of an appeal or other review.

Usually the chairman of the board will open the interview by reviewing the highlights of your education and work experience from your application – primarily for the benefit of the other members of the board, as well as to get the material into the record. Do not interrupt or comment unless there is an error or significant misinterpretation; if that is the case, do not hesitate. But do not quibble about insignificant matters. Also, he will usually ask you some question about your education, experience or your present job – partly to get you to start talking and to establish the interviewing "rapport." He may start the actual questioning, or turn it over to one of the other members. Frequently, each member undertakes the questioning on a particular area, one in which he is perhaps most competent, so you can expect each member to participate in the examination. Because time is limited, you may also expect some rather abrupt switches in the direction the questioning takes, so do not be upset by it. Normally, a board member will not pursue a single line of questioning unless he discovers a particular strength or weakness.

After each member has participated, the chairman will usually ask whether any member has any further questions, then will ask you if you have anything you wish to add. Unless you are expecting this question, it may floor you. Worse, it may start you off on an extended, extemporaneous speech. The board is not usually seeking more information. The question is principally to offer you a last opportunity to present further qualifications or to indicate that you have nothing to add. So, if you feel that a significant qualification or characteristic has been overlooked, it is proper to point it out in a sentence or so. Do not compliment the board on the thoroughness of their examination – they have been sketchy, and you know it. If you wish, merely say, "No thank you, I have nothing further to add." This is a point where you can "talk yourself out" of a good impression or fail to present an important bit of information. Remember, *you close the interview yourself.*

The chairman will then say, "That is all, Mr. _____, thank you." Do not be startled; the interview is over, and quicker than you think. Thank him, gather your belongings and take your leave. Save your sigh of relief for the other side of the door.

How to put your best foot forward

Throughout this entire process, you may feel that the board individually and collectively is trying to pierce your defenses, seek out your hidden weaknesses and embarrass and confuse you. Actually, this is not true. They are obliged to make an appraisal of your qualifications for the job you are seeking, and they want to see you in your best light. Remember, they must interview all candidates and a non-cooperative candidate may become a failure in spite of their best efforts to bring out his qualifications. Here are 15 suggestions that will help you:

1) Be natural – Keep your attitude confident, not cocky

If you are not confident that you can do the job, do not expect the board to be. Do not apologize for your weaknesses, try to bring out your strong points. The board is interested in a positive, not negative, presentation. Cockiness will antagonize any board member and make him wonder if you are covering up a weakness by a false show of strength.

2) Get comfortable, but don't lounge or sprawl

Sit erectly but not stiffly. A careless posture may lead the board to conclude that you are careless in other things, or at least that you are not impressed by the importance of the occasion. Either conclusion is natural, even if incorrect. Do not fuss with your clothing, a pencil or an ashtray. Your hands may occasionally be useful to emphasize a point; do not let them become a point of distraction.

3) Do not wisecrack or make small talk

This is a serious situation, and your attitude should show that you consider it as such. Further, the time of the board is limited – they do not want to waste it, and neither should you.

4) Do not exaggerate your experience or abilities

In the first place, from information in the application or other interviews and sources, the board may know more about you than you think. Secondly, you probably will not get away with it. An experienced board is rather adept at spotting such a situation, so do not take the chance.

5) If you know a board member, do not make a point of it, yet do not hide it

Certainly you are not fooling him, and probably not the other members of the board. Do not try to take advantage of your acquaintanceship – it will probably do you little good.

6) Do not dominate the interview

Let the board do that. They will give you the clues – do not assume that you have to do all the talking. Realize that the board has a number of questions to ask you, and do not try to take up all the interview time by showing off your extensive knowledge of the answer to the first one.

7) Be attentive

You only have 20 minutes or so, and you should keep your attention at its sharpest throughout. When a member is addressing a problem or question to you, give him your undivided attention. Address your reply principally to him, but do not exclude the other board members.

8) Do not interrupt

A board member may be stating a problem for you to analyze. He will ask you a question when the time comes. Let him state the problem, and wait for the question.

9) Make sure you understand the question

Do not try to answer until you are sure what the question is. If it is not clear, restate it in your own words or ask the board member to clarify it for you. However, do not haggle about minor elements.

10) Reply promptly but not hastily

A common entry on oral board rating sheets is "candidate responded readily," or "candidate hesitated in replies." Respond as promptly and quickly as you can, but do not jump to a hasty, ill-considered answer.

11) Do not be peremptory in your answers

A brief answer is proper – but do not fire your answer back. That is a losing game from your point of view. The board member can probably ask questions much faster than you can answer them.

12) Do not try to create the answer you think the board member wants

He is interested in what kind of mind you have and how it works – not in playing games. Furthermore, he can usually spot this practice and will actually grade you down on it.

13) Do not switch sides in your reply merely to agree with a board member

Frequently, a member will take a contrary position merely to draw you out and to see if you are willing and able to defend your point of view. Do not start a debate, yet do not surrender a good position. If a position is worth taking, it is worth defending.

14) Do not be afraid to admit an error in judgment if you are shown to be wrong

The board knows that you are forced to reply without any opportunity for careful consideration. Your answer may be demonstrably wrong. If so, admit it and get on with the interview.

15) Do not dwell at length on your present job

The opening question may relate to your present assignment. Answer the question but do not go into an extended discussion. You are being examined for a *new* job, not your present one. As a matter of fact, try to phrase ALL your answers in terms of the job for which you are being examined.

Basis of Rating

Probably you will forget most of these "do's" and "don'ts" when you walk into the oral interview room. Even remembering them all will not ensure you a passing grade. Perhaps you did not have the qualifications in the first place. But remembering them will help you to put your best foot forward, without treading on the toes of the board members.

Rumor and popular opinion to the contrary notwithstanding, an oral board wants you to make the best appearance possible. They know you are under pressure – but they also want to see how you respond to it as a guide to what your reaction would be under the pressures of the job you seek. They will be influenced by the degree of poise you display, the personal traits you show and the manner in which you respond.

ABOUT THIS BOOK

This book contains tests divided into Examination Sections. Go through each test, answering every question in the margin. We have also attached a sample answer sheet at the back of the book that can be removed and used. At the end of each test look at the answer key and check your answers. On the ones you got wrong, look at the right answer choice and learn. Do not fill in the answers first. Do not memorize the questions and answers, but understand the answer and principles involved. On your test, the questions will likely be different from the samples. Questions are changed and new ones added. If you understand these past questions you should have success with any changes that arise. Tests may consist of several types of questions. We have additional books on each subject should more study be advisable or necessary for you. Finally, the more you study, the better prepared you will be. This book is intended to be the last thing you study before you walk into the examination room. Prior study of relevant texts is also recommended. NLC publishes some of these in our Fundamental Series. Knowledge and good sense are important factors in passing your exam. Good luck also helps. So now study this Passbook, absorb the material contained within and take that knowledge into the examination. Then do your best to pass that exam.

EXAMINATION SECTION

EXAMINATION SECTION
TEST 1

DIRECTIONS: Each question or incomplete statement is followed by several suggested answers or completions. Select the one that BEST answers the question or completes the statement. *PRINT THE LETTER OF THE CORRECT ANSWER IN THE SPACE AT THE RIGHT.*

Questions 1-17.

DIRECTIONS: Questions 1 through 17 are to be answered on the basis of the figure below, a diagram of typical lubrication points on a wheel-mounted hydraulic crane. Place the letter that corresponds to each diagrammed lubrication point in the space at the right.

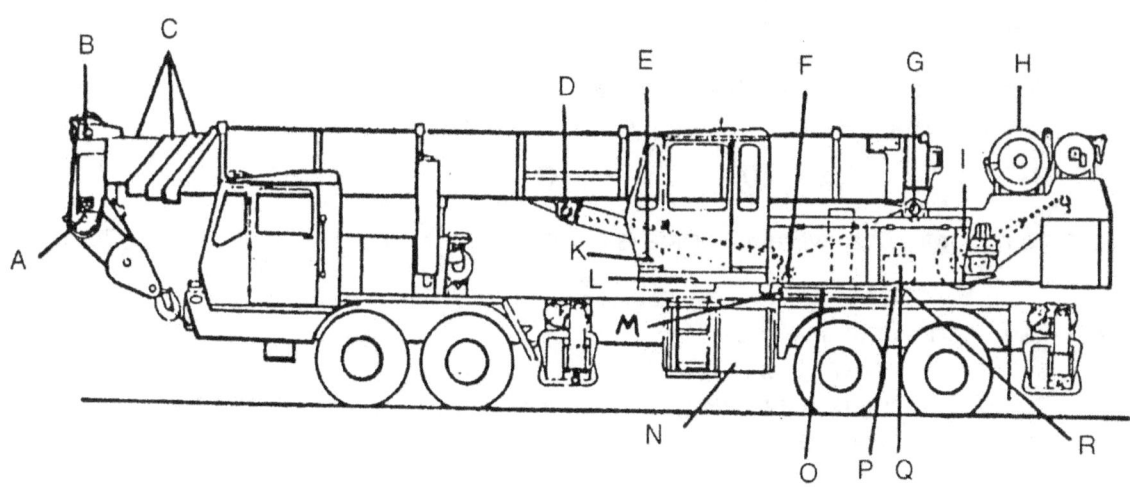

1.	Hoist final drive assembly	1._____
2.	Swing box bearing	2._____
3.	Boom sections	3._____
4.	Pinion	4._____
5.	Hose reel	5._____
6.	Turntable bearing	6._____
7.	Swing brake pedal	7._____
8.	Base lift cylinders	8._____
9.	Swing box gear case	9._____
10.	Hydraulic oil reservoir	10._____
11.	Turntable pinion gear	11._____
12.	Top lift cylinders	12._____

1

13. Brake master cylinder 13.____

14. Boom nose idler sheave 14.____

15. Throttle pedal 15.____

16. Boom nose sheaves 16.____

17. Boom pivot 17.____

18. If oil foams in the reservoir of a crane's hydraulic pump, the MOST likely remedy is to 18.____
    A. fill reservoir to adequate level
    B. clean pump-to-control valve supply line
    C. adjust system relief valve
    D. clear reservoir-to-pump supply line

19. The original filter for a crane's hydraulic system should be replaced after the crane's first 19.____
    _____ hours of operation.
    A. 24　　　　B. 50　　　　C. 100　　　　D. 200

20. If the swing motor of a hydraulic crane is turning in the wrong direction, the MOST likely 20.____
    cause is
    A. damaged output shaft bearing
    B. sticking control valve spool
    C. improper swing brake release
    D. improper port connections

21. What is the ratio of fuel oil to hydraulic oil used in flushing crane systems? 21.____
    A. 1:1　　　　B. 1:3　　　　C. 1:5　　　　D. 2:1

22. If a spur-geared chain hoist will not operate in the hoisting direction, the MOST probable 22.____
    cause is
    A. overload
    B. chain binding
    C. lower load side of chain on wrong side of liftwheel
    D. pawl not engaging with ratchet

23. What is represented by the hydraulic system symbol shown at the right? 23.____
    A. Push-button operation
    B. Connector
    C. Mechanical operation
    D. Check valve

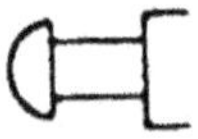

24. What is represented by the hydraulic system symbol shown at the right? 24.____
    A. Pressure relief valve
    B. Fixed restriction
    C. Line to vented manifold
    D. Variable restriction

25. What is represented by the hydraulic system symbol shown at the right?
    A. Single motor, fixed displacement
    B. Reversible motor, variable displacement, reversible
    C. Rotating shaft
    D. Variable displacement pump

25._____

KEY (CORRECT ANSWERS)

1. H
2. R
3. C
4. P
5. J

6. M
7. E
8. F
9. Q
10. N

11. O
12. D
13. M
14. B
15. K

16. A
17. G
18. A
19. B
20. D

21. A
22. B
23. A
24. B
25. C

TEST 2

DIRECTIONS: Each question or incomplete statement is followed by several suggested answers or completions. Select the one that BEST answers the question or completes the statement. *PRINT THE LETTER OF THE CORRECT ANSWER IN THE SPACE AT THE RIGHT.*

Questions 1-25.

DIRECTIONS: In Questions 1 through 25, what is represented by each of the hydraulic system symbols shown?

1.
   A. Flow control valve, adjustable, non-compensated
   B. Manual operation
   C. Pressure gauge
   D. Check valve

   1.____

2.
   A. Differential double-acting cylinder
   B. Non-differential double-acting cylinder
   C. Detent operation
   D. Single-acting cylinder

   2.____

3.
   A. Push-button operation   B. Internal supply pilot pressure
   C. Manual operation   D. Pressure reducing valve

   3.____

4.
   A. Differential double-acting cylinder   B. Manual shut-off valve
   C. Lines passing   D. Flow direction

   4.____

5.
   A. Variable restriction   B. Flexible line
   C. Plugged connection   D. Lines passing

   5.____

6.
   A. Drain line   B. Flow direction
   C. Pilot line   D. Working line

   6.____

2 (#2)

7.

A. Heater
C. Vented reservoir
B. Gas-charged accumulator
D. Connector

8.

A. Cooler
B. Fixed-displacement pump
C. Detent operation
D. Remote supply pilot pressure

9.

A. Filter
C. Manual shut-off valve
B. Temperature control
D. Pressure gauge

10.

A. Lines passing
B. Lines joining
C. Line to reservoir
D. Adjustable flow-control valve, non-compensated

11.

A. Cooler
C. Heater
B. Single-winding solenoid
D. Filter

12.

A. Electric motor
C. Rotating shaft
B. Pressure gauge
D. Reversing motor

13.

A. Nonreversible fixed displacement motor
B. Pressure gauge
C. Pressure relief valve
D. Fixed displacement pump

14.

A. Variable line restriction
B. Line to vented manifold
C. Plug or plugged connection
D. Passing lines

15.

A. Adjustable flow control valve
B. Double-acting non-reversible cylinder
C. Two-position, two-connection valve
D. Valve capable of infinite positioning

16.

A. Pressure compensated operation
B. Spring-loaded accumulator
C. Single-winding solenoid
D. Remote supply pilot pressure

17.

A. Lever operation
B. Manual operation
C. Pressure compensated operation
D. Pedal or treadle operation

18.

A. Single-acting cylinder
B. Temperature controller
C. Non-differential double-acting cylinder
D. Internal supply pilot pressure

19.

A. Plugged connection
C. Line to reservoir
B. Line to vented manifold
D. Vented reservoir

20.

A. Two-position, two-connection valve
B. Two-position, three-connection valve
C. Lines passing
D. Two-position, four-connection valve

21.

A. Electric motor   B. Heater
C. Reversing motor   D. Filter

22.

A. Mechanical operation
B. Enclosure
C. Pressure-compensated operation
D. Detent operation

23.

A. Fixed displacement, non-reversible motor
B. Check valve
C. Fixed displacement pump
D. Variable replacement, reversible motor

24.

A. Vented reservoir   B. Gas-loaded accumulator
C. Enclosure   D. Drain line

25.

A. Plug or plugged connection
B. Direction of flow
C. Connector
D. Line to vented manifold

KEY (CORRECT ANSWERS)

1. D
2. A
3. C
4. B
5. B

6. D
7. B
8. C
9. A
10. A

11. A
12. B
13. D
14. A
15. C

16. C
17. D
18. A
19. B
20. D

21. B
22. C
23. A
24. C
25. A

EXAMINATION SECTION
TEST 1

DIRECTIONS: Each question or incomplete statement is followed by several suggested answers or completions. Select the one that BEST answers the question or completes the statement. *PRINT THE LETTER OF THE CORRECT ANSWER IN THE SPACE AT THE RIGHT.*

Questions 1-15.

DIRECTIONS: Questions 1 through 15 are to be answered on the basis of the figure below, a diagram of the machinery typically found in a mobile crane upperstructure. Place the letter that corresponds to each diagrammed component in the space at the right.

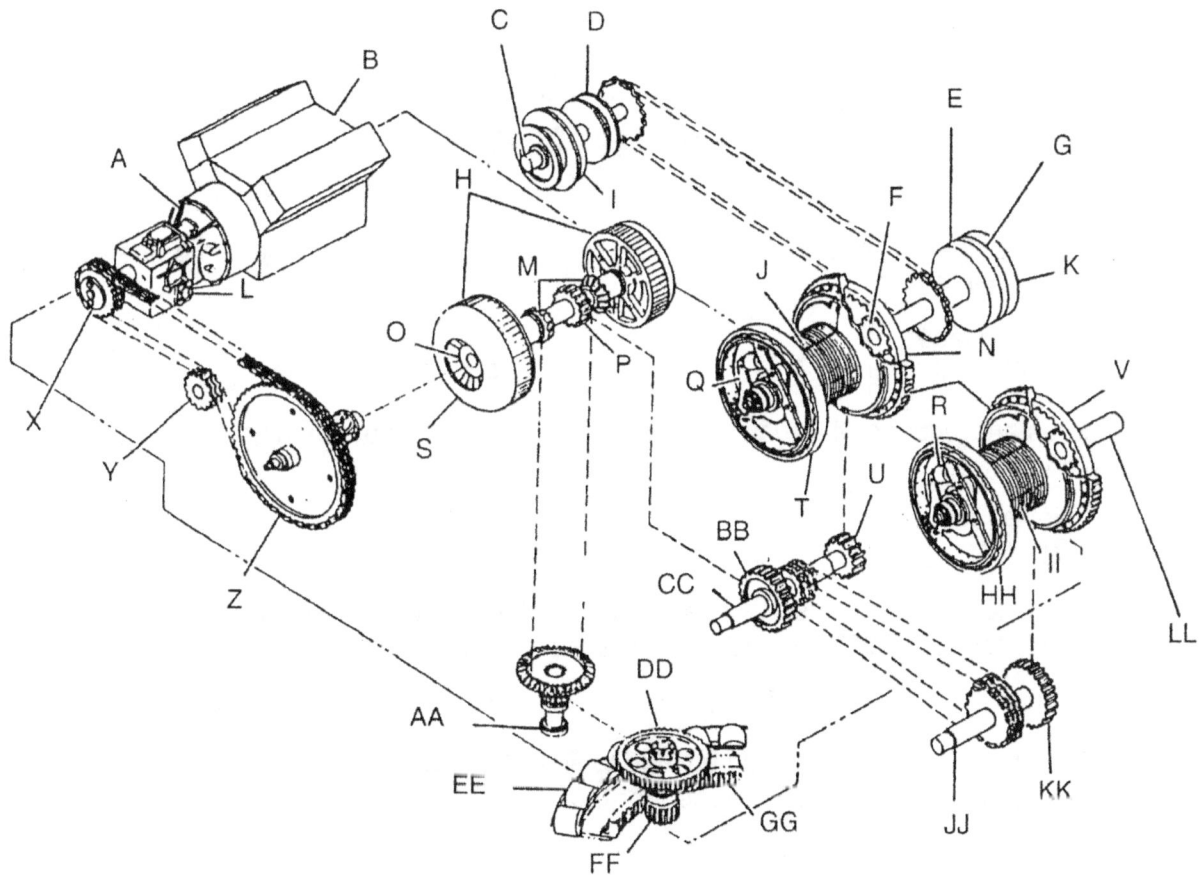

1. Planetary gear   1.____

2. Brake band surface   2.____

3. Magnetorque sprocket   3.____

4. Swing shaft pinion   4.____

5. Jack shaft   5.____

6. Engine clutch   6.____

9

7. Boom hoist clutch   7._____

8. Swing gear   8._____

9. Engine transmission or torque converter   9._____

10. Planetary pinion   10._____

11. Front drum   11._____

12. Outer drum drive pinion   12._____

13. Engine sprocket   13._____

14. Rear drum clutch   14._____

15. Intermediate reduction shaft   15._____

16. To ensure that all sections of a telescoping boom are thoroughly lubricated, the boom should be extended and brushed with _____-type lubricant.   16._____

    A. CG   B. EP   C. WGL   D. OG

17. If the hook of an all-electric chain hoist lowers when the hoisting control is operated, the probable cause is   17._____

    A. low voltage   B. brake dragging
    C. open control circuit   D. phase failure

18. Records are required of visual inspections made of hoists operating under _____ service conditions.   18._____

    A. infrequent   B. normal
    C. heavy   D. severe

19. The rated load of a rope used with an electric hoist, divided by the parts of the rope used in the hoist, should NOT exceed _____% of the nominal breaking strength of the rope.   19._____

    A. 20   B. 40   C. 55   D. 75

20. An electric hoist's brakes should be able to slow the load descent by AT LEAST _____% of the rated lowering speed for the load.   20._____

    A. 30   B. 75   C. 100   D. 120

21. How often should the bolts used to attach boom mountings be inspected, regardless of use?   21._____

    A. Daily   B. Weekly   C. Monthly   D. Bimonthly

22. Normal operation of a chain hoist is defined as operation with uniform loads up to _____% of capacity during a single work shift.   22._____

    A. 25   B. 45   C. 65   D. 85

23. Inspection of hoists under severe operation should occur   23._____

    A. daily   B. daily to weekly
    C. weekly to monthly   D. monthly

24. If the jack cylinder of a hydraulic outrigger retracts under a load, each of the following is a possible remedy EXCEPT 24.____

    A. replace cylinder seals
    B. replace valve assembly
    C. add hydraulic oil to reservoir
    D. replace cylinder

25. Which of the following operations involved in aligning and servicing a telescoping boom would occur FIRST? 25.____

    A. Turn adjusting screws snug against boom section
    B. Adjust side wear pads snug against boom section
    C. Retract boom sections to align high point on boom section
    D. Lubricate boom completely

KEY (CORRECT ANSWERS)

1.	N	11.	II
2.	HH	12.	P
3.	Z	13.	X
4.	FF	14.	Q
5.	JJ	15.	CC
6.	A	16.	B
7.	K	17.	D
8.	GG	18.	A
9.	L	19.	A
10.	F	20.	D

21. A
22. C
23. B
24. C
25. D

TEST 2

DIRECTIONS: Each question or incomplete statement is followed by several suggested answers or completions. Select the one that BEST answers the question or completes the statement. *PRINT THE LETTER OF THE CORRECT ANSWER IN THE SPACE AT THE RIGHT.*

Questions 1-14.

DIRECTIONS: Questions 1 through 14 are to be answered on the basis of the figure below, a diagram of a typical control valve assembly for a hydraulic crane. Place the letter that corresponds to each diagrammed component in the space at the right.

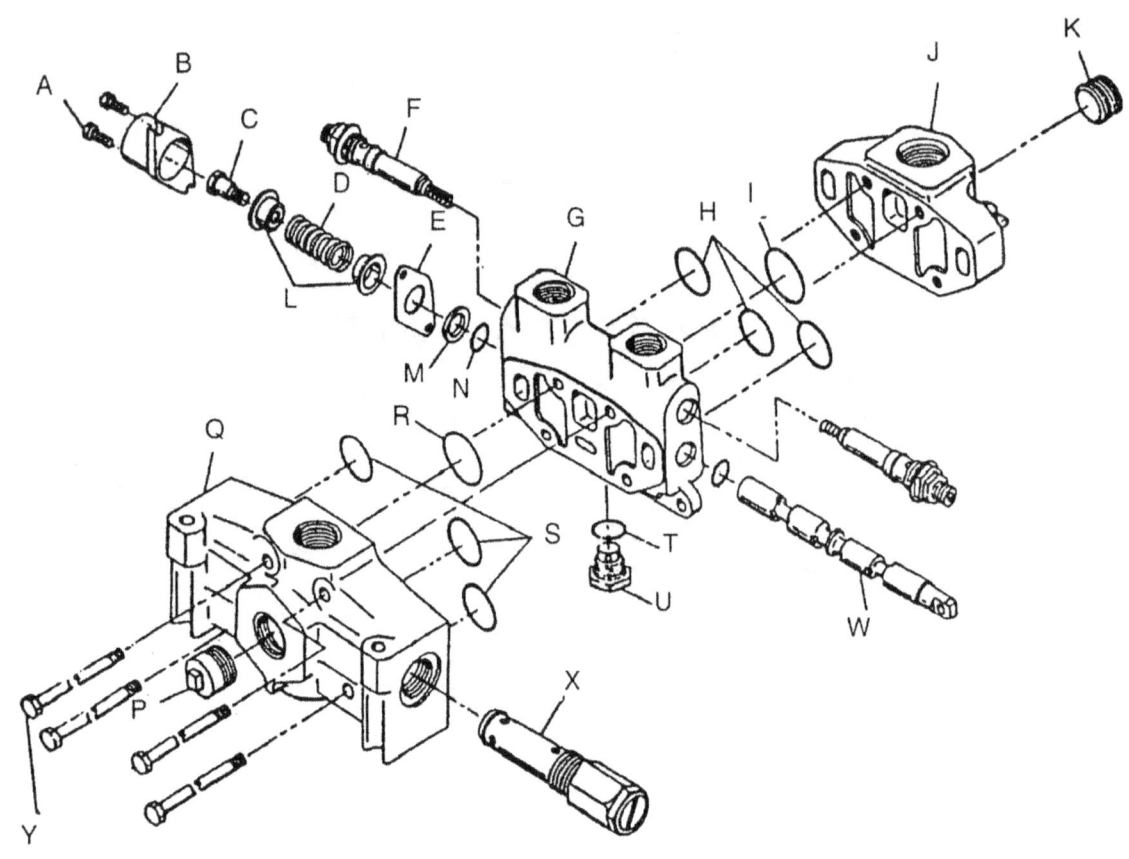

1. Spring guide 1.____

2. Inlet section 2.____

3. Spring 3.____

4. Circuit relief valve 4.____

5. Housing 5.____

6. Backup ring 6.____

7. Tie bolt 7.____

12

8. Ring seal 8.____

9. Outlet relief 9.____

10. Spool 10.____

11. Cap screw 11.____

12. Load check valve 12.____

13. Main relief valve 13.____

14. Retaining plate 14.____

15. Which of the following operations involved in flushing a crane's hydraulic circulatory system would occur LAST? 15.____

    A. Fill reservoir with fuel oil/hydraulic oil solution
    B. Return crane to stowed-boom position
    C. Flush
    D. Cycle crane through all hydraulic functions

16. Inspection of hoists under normal operation should occur 16.____

    A. daily   B. daily to weekly
    C. weekly to monthly   D. monthly

17. If the spool of a hydraulic crane's control valve is sticking, each of the following is a possible remedy EXCEPT 17.____

    A. retorque   B. replace pump
    C. clear pipe line   D. flush system

18. Which of the following conditions could cause a failure of hydraulic outriggers to set? 18.____

    A. Cracked piston
    B. Low hydraulic oil
    C. Improper activation sequence
    D. Damaged hydraulic cylinder

19. If a crane's hydraulic pump is not delivering fluid, each of the following is a possible cause EXCEPT 19.____

    A. sheared coupling
    B. internal contamination
    C. system relief valve set too high
    D. air entering at suction manifold

20. The voltage at an electric hoist's pendant push buttons should NOT exceed _____ V for a unit using alternating current. 20.____

    A. 75   B. 150   C. 225   D. 300

21. Which of the following conditions could cause a crane load to drop when the hydraulic control valve spool is moved from neutral?   21.____

    A. Excessive back pressure
    B. Valve cap binding
    C. Dirt in relief valve
    D. Dirt in check valve

22. If a hydraulic crane's boom swing is erratic in either direction, which of the following is NOT a possible remedy?   22.____

    A. Level machine
    B. Replace relief valve
    C. Replace swing motor
    D. Retorque turntable bolts

23. Electric hoists should be clearly marked with each of the following power supply quantities EXCEPT   23.____

    A. resistance
    B. phase
    C. frequency
    D. voltage

24. If a hydraulic crane's solenoid valve shows external leakage, which of the following is NOT a likely cause?   24.____

    A. Damaged quad rings
    B. Pressure in excess of valve rating
    C. Loose tie bolts
    D. Damaged solenoid

25. Inspection of hoists under heavy operation should occur   25.____

    A. daily
    B. daily to weekly
    C. weekly to monthly
    D. monthly

KEY (CORRECT ANSWERS)

1.	L	11.	A
2.	Q	12.	U
3.	D	13.	X
4.	F	14.	E
5.	G	15.	C
6.	M	16.	D
7.	Y	17.	B
8.	V	18.	C
9.	J	19.	C
10.	W	20.	B

21. D
22. A
23. A
24. B
25. C

EXAMINATION SECTION
TEST 1

DIRECTIONS: Each question or incomplete statement is followed by several suggested answers or completions. Select the one that BEST answers the question or completes the statement. *PRINT THE LETTER OF THE CORRECT ANSWER IN THE SPACE AT THE RIGHT.*

1. To permit both vertical wheel displacement and an equalization of loading on the wheels of a crane, a rigger must assemble a   1.____

   A. barrel   B. dog   C. horse   D. bogie

2. What type of erection assembly has a vertical mast that is shorter than its boom?   2.____

   A. High lift
   C. Gantry crane
   B. Stiff-leg derrick
   D. Guy derrick

3. Typically, how many drums are required to provide power to the main hoisting cable on the upperstructure of a cable-controlled crane?   3.____

   A. 1   B. 2   C. 3   D. 4

4. The approximate load limit, at a horizontal load radius of 40 feet, for a 25-ton crane using a multi-part hoist line is _____ pounds.   4.____

   A. 10,000   B. 17,000   C. 28,000   D. 36,000

5. To reduce the unit bearing pressure on the supporting surface, _____ are typically placed beneath mobile crane tracks or outrigger floats.   5.____

   A. backstays
   C. pendants
   B. cribbing
   D. footblocks

6. Which of the following cross-sectional shapes is NOT normally used in the design of concentric sections of a telescoping boom?   6.____

   A. Triangular
   C. Rectangular
   B. Round
   D. Trapezoidal

7. What type of jib boom is used to extend the maximum height of tower cranes that are mounted on slewing platforms?   7.____

   A. Chicago   B. Saddle   C. Lift   D. Luffing

8. Generally, the MAXIMUM load for the smallest tower crane unit with a horizontal jib at a 30-foot radius is considered to be _____ tons.   8.____

   A. 2   B. 12   C. 35   D. 60

9. What is the lift capacity of a heavy-duty wire rope air hoist?   9.____

   A. 750 pounds
   C. 5 tons
   B. 1 ton
   D. 15 tons

10. According to the PCSA standard, the rated load limit of a wheel-mounted crane is _____% of the machine's tipping load.   10.____

    A. 65   B. 75   C. 85   D. 95

15

11. The point of contact between the rope and drum where the rope changes layers is known as the

    A. flange point B. float
    C. whip D. fleet point

12. The line speed of cranes USUALLY ranges between _____ feet/minute.

    A. 80-125 B. 150-170 C. 150-225 D. 175-300

13. Which of the following is NOT typically carried by the counter jib on a tower crane assembly using a saddle jib?

    A. Counterweights B. Power plant
    C. Load winch D. Pendant anchors

14. Which of the following functions should typically be mechanically driven, rather than hydraulically?

    A. Load hoist B. Travel
    C. Boom hoist D. Load swing

15. The type of mobile crane that offers the GREATEST stability on natural ground is the

    A. rough-terrain B. truck-mounted
    C. high-lift D. crawler

16. The term for the angle between the centerline of a jib and the centerline of the boom on which it is mounted is _____ angle.

    A. swing B. offset C. topping D. fleet

17. At a load radius of 100 feet, a gantry crane can handle up to _____ tons.

    A. 15 B. 40 C. 60 D. 80

18. To calculate the safety of total bearing for a mobile crane, each of the following factors must be known EXCEPT

    A. area of crane contacting surface
    B. load capacity of lift line
    C. bearing capacity of earth surface
    D. total loaded weight of crane

19. The lifting capacity of the largest gin poles is about _____ tons.

    A. 80 B. 150 C. 300 D. 500

20. The rope used for erection purposes is MOST commonly made from

    A. mild plow steel B. crucible cast steel
    C. iron D. improved plow steel

21. The common 6 x 19 lift line, with a diameter of 1/2 inch and a safety factor of 4.0, can safely lift APPROXIMATELY _____ ton(s).

    A. 1 B. 2.5 C. 5 D. 7.5

22. A guy derrick system uses guy lines that are USUALLY _____ inches in diameter.   22.____

    A. 1/2-1   B. 1-1 1/2   C. 1 1/2-2   D. 2-2 1/2

23. If an all-electric chain hoist will not operate at slow speed in either direction, the MOST likely cause is   23.____

    A. open circuit
    B. inoperative limit switches
    C. extreme external heat
    D. brake dragging

24. What type of crane typically uses a knuckleboom?   24.____

    A. Crawler   B. Tower
    C. Truck-mounted   D. Gantry

25. A fully extended high-lift telescoping boom, with an added jib, has a MAXIMUM reach of approximately _____ feet.   25.____

    A. 80-90   B. 90-110   C. 110-130   D. 130-140

KEY (CORRECT ANSWERS)

1. D   11. A
2. B   12. B
3. B   13. D
4. B   14. A
5. B   15. D

6. A   16. B
7. D   17. B
8. A   18. B
9. D   19. C
10. B   20. D

21. B
22. C
23. A
24. C
25. D

TEST 2

DIRECTIONS: Each question or incomplete statement is followed by several suggested answers or completions. Select the one that BEST answers the question or completes the statement. *PRINT THE LETTER OF THE CORRECT ANSWER IN THE SPACE AT THE RIGHT.*

1. Guy ropes attach to a fitting mounted at the top of a derrick mast known as a(n)

   A. spider   B. topping   C. tackle   D. rooster

2. Which of the following types of cranes is mounted on a single-engine, self-propelled wheel mounting?

   A. Rough-terrain   B. Crawler
   C. High-lift   D. Truck-mounted

3. The _____ sheave is used to prevent excessive fleet angle during crane operation.

   A. drum   B. plain bore
   C. self-lubricating   D. fleeting

4. Which of the following earth surfaces has a bearing capacity of about 12 tons per square foot?

   A. Hard, sound rock   B. Hardpan over rock
   C. Soft rock   D. Compact clay/sand/gravel

5. The telescoping boom typically has a MAXIMUM working radius of _____ feet.

   A. 17   B. 24   C. 45   D. 72

6. What type of erection equipment is considered to be MOST economical in terms of cost per pound hoisted?

   A. Stiff-leg derrick   B. Tower crane
   C. Truck-mounted crane   D. Guy derrick

7. According to SAE standards, the load hoist drums of a cable-controlled crane must have a diameter of AT LEAST _____ times the nominal diameter of the rope line used with them.

   A. 12   B. 15   C. 18   D. 21

8. A fully extended high-lift telescoping boom has a maximum reach of approximately _____ feet.

   A. 80-90   B. 90-110   C. 110-130   D. 130-140

9. Which of the following is NOT a factor used to determine the stability of a loaded crawler crane?

   A. Boom weight   B. Load carrying capacity
   C. Lift angle   D. Load radius

10. A _____ is mounted to the base of a derrick mast to receive and guide the ropes used for swinging.

    A. butt section
    B. foot mast
    C. footblock
    D. bull wheel

11. What is the typical lift capacity of a hand-chain hoist?

    A. 800 pounds
    B. 5 tons
    C. 25 tons
    D. 50 tons

12. When outriggers are used on a mobile crane, the wheels or crawler tracks within the smallest radius containing the outriggers must be relieved of _____ % of the weight by outrigger jacks or blocking.

    A. 50 B. 70 C. 85 D. 100

13. What type of tower crane mounting, consisting of a steel-legged structure that adds little support weight, is used when passage beneath the crane is necessary, or when the crane travels on rails?

    A. Portal B. Gantry C. Revolver D. Overhead

14. _____ stability is NOT one of the stability factors that must be checked before placing a tower crane into service.

    A. Basic
    B. Rated
    C. Dynamic
    D. Extreme load

15. If the hook of an all-electric chain hoist fails to stop at either or both ends of travel, each of the following is a possible cause EXCEPT

    A. shaft not rotating
    B. open circuit
    C. limit switch failure
    D. loose guide plate

16. The PCSA requires that for mobile cranes, the weight bearing down on all wheels, outriggers, crawler tracks or idlers on the side or end of the undercarriage supporting the least load shall NOT be less than _____% of the total weight of the crane.

    A. 5 B. 10 C. 15 D. 20

17. The measure for stability against backward tipping of a truck- or wheel-mounted crane is based on all wheels on the side of the carrier under the loaded side/end of the crane taking AT LEAST _____ % of the weight of the equipment.

    A. 5 B. 15 C. 25 D. 35

18. Where space between buildings does not allow the back projecting part of a tower crane jib to extend, the lift-loading jib can be balanced by

    A. gantry-type backstay
    B. free-hanging counterweight
    C. outriggers
    D. luffing jib

19. A two-part line allows approximately _____ the lifting speed of a single line.

    A. the same as   B. one-half
    C. twice   D. three times

20. Which special tower crane mounting is a fixed structure to which the crane's slewing ring is attached?

    A. Portal   B. Pedestal   C. Overhead   D. Gantry

21. According to the PCSA standard, the rated load limit of a crane using outriggers is _____ % of the machine's tipping load.

    A. 65   B. 75   C. 85   D. 95

22. Derrick booms are swung by _____ lines reeved to the boom.

    A. winch   B. sill   C. tag   D. vang

23. The highest working vertical angle of a telescoping boom is APPROXIMATELY _____.

    A. 30   B. 45   C. 60   D. 80

24. The approximate load limit, at a horizontal load radius of 20 feet, for a 60-ton crane using a multi-part hoist line is _____ pounds.

    A. 15,000   B. 25,000   C. 40,000   D. 55,000

25. For a cable-controlled crane with a latticed boom that requires an additional drum for raising and lowering the boom, the boom hoist diameter must be AT LEAST _____ times the nominal diameter of the rope line used with it.

    A. 12   B. 15   C. 18   D. 21

EXAMINATION SECTION
TEST 1

DIRECTIONS: Each question or incomplete statement is followed by several suggested answers or completions. Select the one that BEST answers the question or completes the statement. *PRINT THE LETTER OF THE CORRECT ANSWER IN THE SPACE AT THE RIGHT.*

Questions 1-9.

DIRECTIONS: Questions 1 through 9 refer to the figure below, a diagram of hand signals used in rigging and hoisting operations. Place the letter that corresponds to each diagrammed signal in the space at the right.

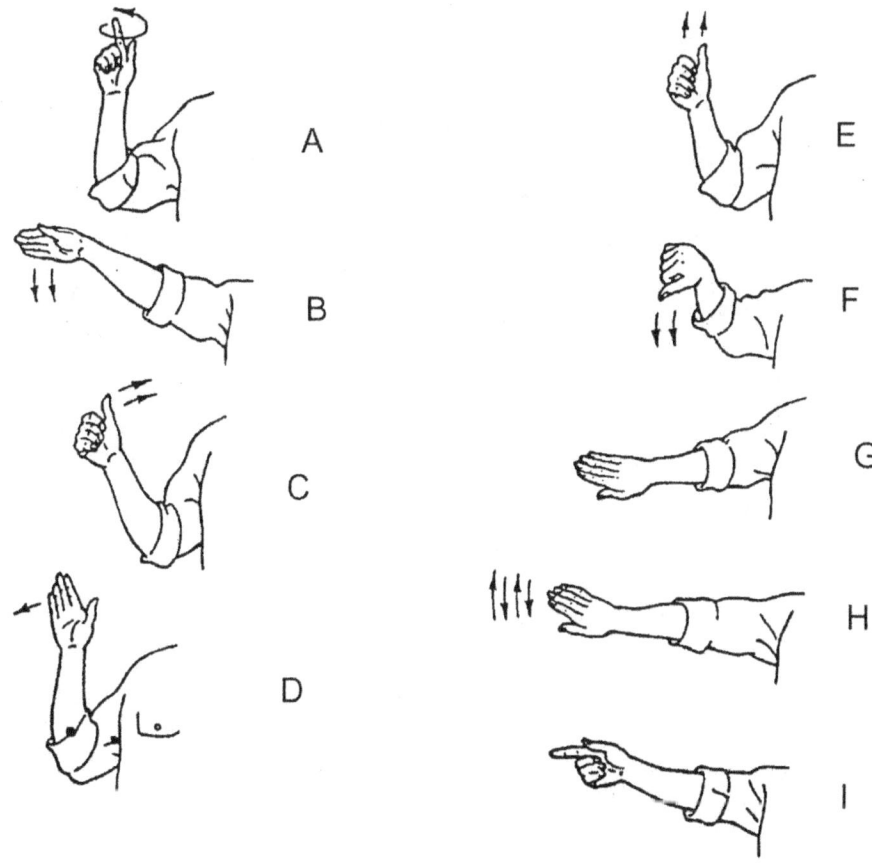

1. Boom up   1._____
2. Slew boom   2._____
3. Stop   3._____
4. Rack trolley   4._____
5. Lower load   5._____

6. Boom down 6._____

7. Emergency stop 7._____

8. Travel crane bridge or caterpillar 8._____

9. Hoist load 9._____

Questions 10-17.

DIRECTIONS: Questions 10 through 17 refer to the figure below, a diagram of a typical crane operating cycle. Place the letter that corresponds to each diagrammed component in the space at the right.

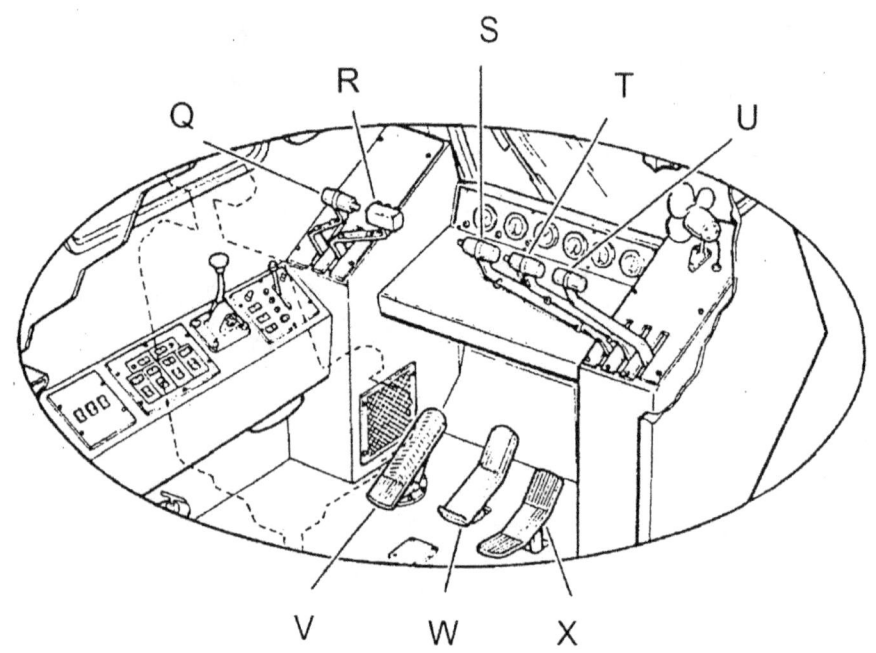

10. Main winch lever 10._____

11. Boom hoist pedal 11._____

12. Telescope lever 12._____

13. Engine throttle pedal 13._____

14. Boom hoist lever 14._____

15. Swing brake pedal 15._____

16. Swing lever 16._____

17. Auxiliary winch lever 17._____

18. A wire rope used with cranes or derricks must be removed from service when _____ the original diameter of the outside individual wires is worn. 18._____

    A. 1/8   B. 1/5   C. 1/3   D. 1/2

19. Each of the following is a type of heavy-lift attachment used with mobile cranes EXCEPT   19._____
    A. trailing counterweight   B. luffing jib
    C. guy derrick   D. ring system

20. A guy derrick system provides a mast with AT LEAST _____ guy lines.   20._____
    A. 6   B. 8   C. 10   D. 12

21. Truck-mounted booms are typically used for loads that do NOT exceed _____ tons.   21._____
    A. 5-10   B. 10-20   C. 15-30   D. 20-35

22. If a spur-geared hoist will not hold a load in suspension, each of the following is a possible cause EXCEPT   22._____
    A. broken or worn ratchet teeth
    B. deformed lift wheel teeth
    C. worn brake parts
    D. lower hook or load side of chain on wrong side of liftwheel

23. The MAXIMUM rate for swinging a load with a crane structure is typically set at   23._____
    A. 2   B. 4   C. 7   D. 15

24. What type of erection equipment has the LARGEST angle between its topping lift line and boom?   24._____
    A. Stiff-leg derrick   B. Tower crane
    C. Truck-mounted crane   D. Guy derrick

25. The telescoping boom has a load capacity of APPROXIMATELY _____ pounds.   25._____
    A. 25,000   B. 45,000   C. 70,000   D. 100,000

KEY (CORRECT ANSWERS)

1. E
2. I
3. G
4. C
5. B

6. F
7. H
8. D
9. A
10. T

11. X
12. R
13. V
14. U
15. W

16. Q
17. S
18. C
19. B
20. C

21. B
22. B
23. B
24. D
25. C

———

TEST 2

DIRECTIONS: Each question or incomplete statement is followed by several suggested answers or completions. Select the one that BEST answers the question or completes the statement. *PRINT THE LETTER OF THE CORRECT ANSWER IN THE SPACE AT THE RIGHT.*

1. Equipment or machines in transit, with no load and boom lowered, must maintain a minimum clearance of AT LEAST _____ feet between electric lines rated between 50 to 345 kV and any part of the crane.

    A. 4   B. 8   C. 10   D. 16

2. According to the PCSA (Power Crane and Shovel Association), the load capacity of a mobile crane is between _____ % of the crane's tipping load in the direction of least stability.

    A. 45-55   B. 55-75   C. 65-85   D. 75-90

3. A wire running rope used with cranes or derricks must be removed from service when there are _____ randomly distributed broken wires in one lay.

    A. 1   B. 3   C. 6   D. 9

4. Which of the following earth surfaces has a bearing capacity of about 4 tons per square foot?

    A. Loose sandy gravel   B. Hardpan over rock
    C. Stiff clay   D. Compact fine sand

5. For most mobile cranes, the MINIMUM load radius is approximately _____ feet.

    A. 8   B. 12   C. 20   D. 24

6. A configuration of two gin poles with a horizontal beam across its pole heads is known as a(n)

    A. A-frame   B. guy derrick
    C. basket derrick   D. gallows frame

7. The approximate load limit, at a horizontal load radius of 30 feet, for a 12 1/2-ton crane using a 2-part hoist line is _____ pounds.

    A. 10,000   B. 17,000   C. 24,000   D. 36,000

8. What is the term used to denote any lines that travel over drums or sheaves?

    A. Load falls   B. Running lines
    C. Guy lines   D. Standing lines

9. Equipment or machines in transit, with no load and boom lowered, must maintain a minimum clearance of AT LEAST _____ feet between electric lines rated between 345 to 750 kV and any part of the crane.

    A. 4   B. 8   C. 10   D. 16

10. Which of the following earth surfaces has a bearing capacity of about 1 ton per square foot?

    A. Soft rock
    B. Firm sandy gravel
    C. Medium sand
    D. Soft clay

11. Most gin poles should NOT typically lean to a vertical angle greater than _____°.

    A. 5   B. 10   C. 15   D. 30

12. A wire rope used with cranes or derricks with a diameter of 7/8" to 1 1/8" must be removed from service when its nominal diameter is reduced more than _____ inch.

    A. 1/64   B. 1/32   C. 3/64   D. 1/16

13. Which type of mobile crane is BEST suited for heavy lifting without much movement?

    A. Rough-terrain
    B. Truck-mounted
    C. High-lift
    D. Crawler

14. The total load capacity for MOST luffing tower cranes is _____ tons.

    A. 12   B. 24   C. 35   D. 45

15. The MOST maneuverable of all erection equipment is the _____ crane.

    A. truck-mounted
    B. crawler
    C. gantry
    D. wheeled

16. What is the lift capacity of a heavy-duty link chain air hoist?

    A. 500 pounds
    B. 1 ton
    C. 3 tons
    D. 8 tons

17. Which of the following earth surfaces has a bearing capacity of about 2 tons per square foot?

    A. Hardpan over rock
    B. Firm sandy gravel
    C. Medium clay
    D. Compact clay/sand/gravel

18. Equipment or machines in transit, with no load and boom lowered, must maintain a minimum clearance of AT LEAST _____ feet between electric lines rated less than 50 kV and any part of the crane.

    A. 4   B. 8   C. 10   D. 16

19. Generally, the maximum load for the largest tower crane unit with a horizontal jib at a 110-foot radius is considered to be _____ tons.

    A. 2   B. 12   C. 35   D. 60

20. The load-moment-indicator system of a crane is typically used to monitor each of the following functions EXCEPT

    A. drum rotation
    B. boom angle
    C. working quadrant
    D. telescoping boom length

21. According to the PCSA standard, the rated load limit of a crawler crane is _____ % of the machine's tipping load.

    A. 65   B. 75   C. 85   D. 95

22. For maximum tower crane loads, the lifting speed is GENERALLY _____ feet per minute.

    A. 10-20   B. 30-40   C. 45-55   D. 65-70

23. Which of the following types of tower crane mountings is MOST versatile?

    A. Static base
    B. Climbing base
    C. Saddle jib
    D. Traveling base

24. Mobile cranes with the shortest booms are limited in their reach for heavy loads to within a radius of approximately _____ feet.

    A. 12   B. 17   C. 24   D. 35

25. If the hook of an all-electric chain hoist will lower but not raise, each of the following is a possible cause EXCEPT

    A. phase failure
    B. excessive load
    C. wrong voltage
    D. inoperative motor reversing switch

KEY (CORRECT ANSWERS)

1. C
2. C
3. C
4. A
5. B

6. D
7. B
8. B
9. D
10. D

11. B
12. D
13. D
14. C
15. B

16. C
17. C
18. A
19. D
20. A

21. B
22. B
23. B
24. B
25. C

EXAMINATION SECTION
TEST 1

DIRECTIONS: Each question or incomplete statement is followed by several suggested answers or completions. Select the one that BEST answers the question or completes the statement. *PRINT THE LETTER OF THE CORRECT ANSWER IN THE SPACE AT THE RIGHT.*

1. A meter is, in inches,
    A. 39.07   B. 39.17   C. 39.27   D. 39.37

2. A metric ton (1000 kg) is, in pounds,
    A. 2000   B. 2040   C. 2140   D. 2240

3. The rule of thumb formula for the safe working load for wire rope is, in tons, (rope diameter)x(rope diameter)x _____.
    A. 2   B. 4   C. 6   D. 8

4. One horsepower is equal to, in foot pounds per second,
    A. 220   B. 330   C. 440   D. 550

5. Of the following, galvanized wire rope would most likely be used for
    A. slings
    B. guy lines
    C. running lines on cranes
    D. topping lines on cranes

6. The type of wire needed to whip the ends of a steel wire cable should be
    A. soft and tempered
    B. soft and annealed
    C. hard and tempered
    D. hard and annealed

7. A birdcage is a
    A. type of knot
    B. type of scaffold
    C. defect in wire rope
    D. defect in manila rope

8. When the crane is not lifting, to be certain the rope on the drum spools evenly, the tension in the rope at the drum should be
    A. 0
    B. 10% of the safe working load
    C. 30% of the safe working load
    D. 50% of the safe working load

9. A disadvantage in using two triple blocks to hoist material is that
    A. they are difficult to assemble
    B. the rope is subject to abrasion
    C. triple blocks are difficult to procure
    D. it raises the load slowly

10. The luffing system on a derrick arrangement is used to
    A. raise or lower the boom   B. swing the boom
    C. raise or lower a load   D. alter the boom length

11.

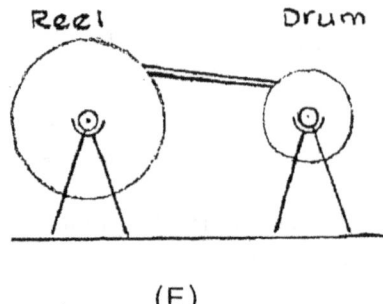
(E)

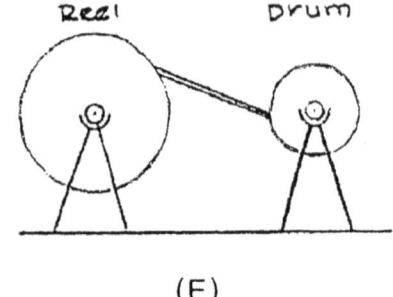
(F)

The sketches shown above show two ways to transfer wire rope from reel to drum. Of the following statements related to the above methods, the one that is correct is Method
    A. E is *correct* because it keeps the coil in the rope unchanged
    B. F is *correct* because it tends to straighten the rope
    C. E is *correct* because it keeps tension in the rope while unreeling
    D. F is *correct* because it prevents the reel from toppling

12.

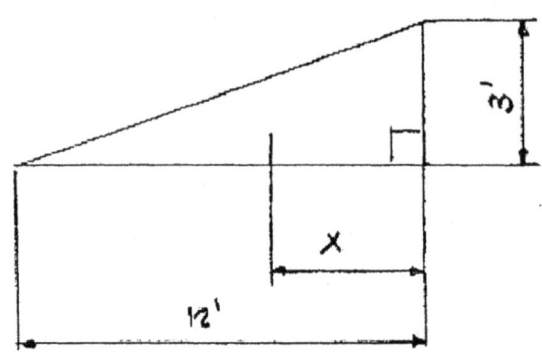

The vertical line marked e.g. goes through the center of gravity of the right triangle. The distance x, in feet, is MOST NEARLY
    A. 3   B. 4   C. 5   D. 6

13. One kip is equal to, in pounds,
    A. 100   B. 1,000   C. 2,000   D. 10,000

14. The specific gravity of aluminum is 2.6. The weight of one cubic foot of aluminum is MOST NEARLY _____ pounds.
    A. 165   B. 180   C. 195   D. 210

15. The type of steel now used to make cable wire is _____ steel.
    A. crucible   B. plow
    C. structural   D. boron

16. The mechanical advantage of the system shown at the right, neglecting friction, is _____ to 1.

   A. 4
   B. 8
   C. 12
   D. 16

16.____

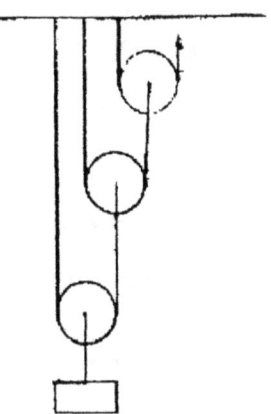

17. The MAIN advantage of a 6 x 19 wire rope over a 6 x 7 wire rope is that the 6 x 19 wire rope is

   A. less expensive
   C. more durable
   B. much stronger
   D. more flexible

17.____

18.

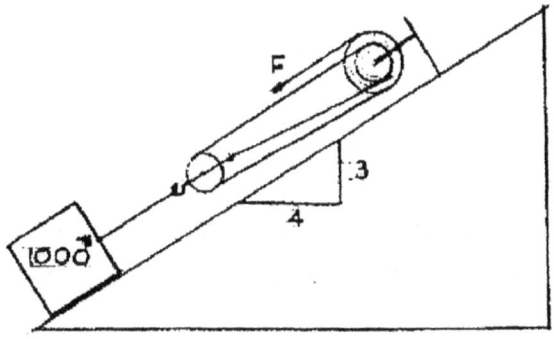

The minimum force F, in pounds, needed to move the 1000 pound load, neglecting friction, is
   A. 200   B. 270   C. 330   D. 350

18.____

19. If a hook is badly overloaded, it would most likely show up on the hook as

   A. a crack in the saddle of the hook
   B. a crack on the underside of the hook
   C. wear in the saddle of the hook
   D. the throat will open beyond the new dimension

19.____

Questions 20-22.

DIRECTIONS: Questions 20 through 22 refer to the diagram below.

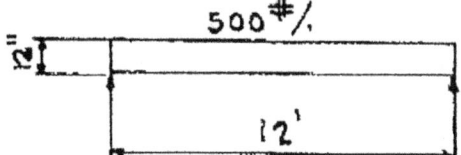

20. The maximum horizontal shearing stress on the 4x12 wood bean is, in pounds per square inch, MOST NEARLY

    A. 63   B. 73   C. 84   D. 94

21. The moment at the center of the beam is, in foot pounds, MOST NEARLY

    A. 6000   B. 7000   C. 8000   D. 9000

22. The maximum bending stress at the center of the beam is, in pounds per square inch, MOST NEARLY

    A. 750   B. 875   C. 1000   D. 1125

23.

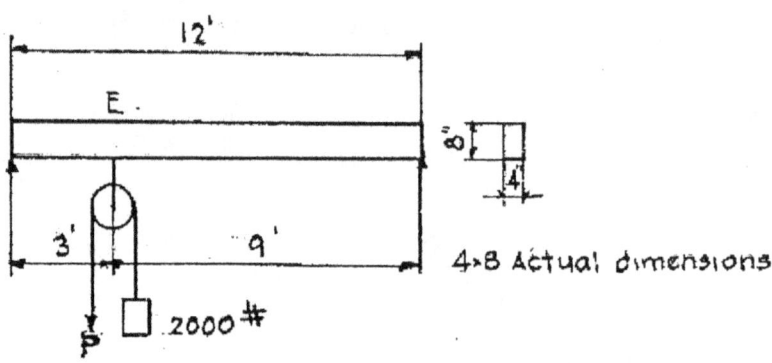

Neglecting the weight of the 4x8 wood beam and the friction resistance in the pulley, the maximum bending stress in the bean is, in pounds per square inch, MOST NEARLY

   A. 1900   B. 2100   C. 2300   D. 2500

Questions 24-25.

DIRECTIONS: Questions 24 and 25 refer to the following diagram.

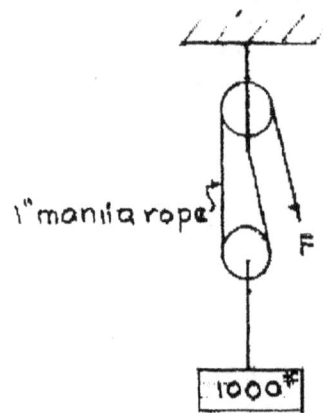

The friction loss over a sheave is 10%

Allowable working load of 1" manila rope is 1000#

24. The minimum load in the lead line F needed to raise the 1000# load taking friction losses into consideration is, in pounds, MOST NEARLY

    A. 500   B. 580   C. 605   D. 635

25. Removing the 1000# load, the maximum load that this system can safely lift is, in pounds, MOST NEARLY

    A. 1210   B. 1580   C. 1710   D. 1830

KEY (CORRECT ANSWERS)

1. D
2. D
3. D
4. D
5. B

6. B
7. C
8. B
9. D
10. A

11. A
12. B
13. B
14. A
15. B

16. B
17. D
18. A
19. D
20. D

21. D
22. D
23. D
24. C
25. C

TEST 2

DIRECTIONS: Each question or incomplete statement is followed by several suggested answers or completions. Select the one that BEST answers the question or completes the statement. *PRINT THE LETTER OF THE CORRECT ANSWER IN THE SPACE AT THE RIGHT.*

Questions 1-3.

DIRECTIONS: Questions 1 through 3 refer to the diagram below. T

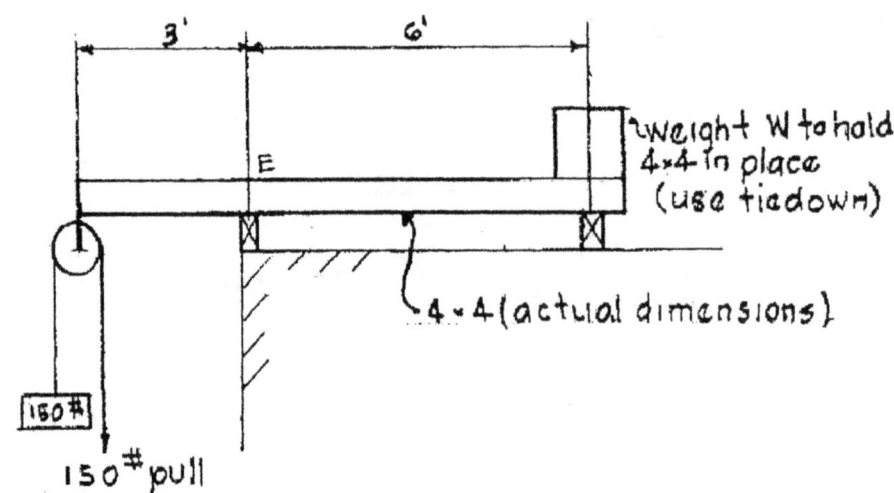

1. Neglecting the weight of the 4x4 wood beam, the weight W needed to hold the 4x4 in place with a factor of safety of 2 is, in pounds, MOST NEARLY

    A. 200   B. 300   C. 400   D. 600

1.____

2. Neglecting the weight of the 4x4 wood beam, the moment on the beam at E is, in foot pounds, MOST NEARLY

    A. 450   B. 600   C. 900   D. 1200

2.____

3. Neglecting the weight of the 4x4 wood beam, the maximum stress due to bending is, in pounds per square inch, MOST NEARLY

    A. 800   B. 900   C. 1000   D. 1200

3.____

4. Of the following hitches, the one that is a choker hitch is

4.____

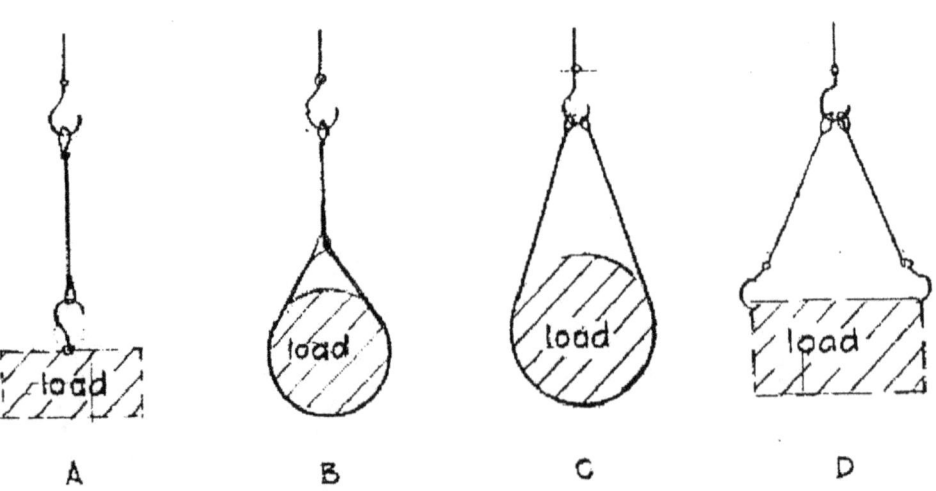

5. The load in the wire rope due to the 2000 pound weight is, in pounds, MOST NEARLY
   A. 1000
   B. 1050
   C. 1100
   D. 1150

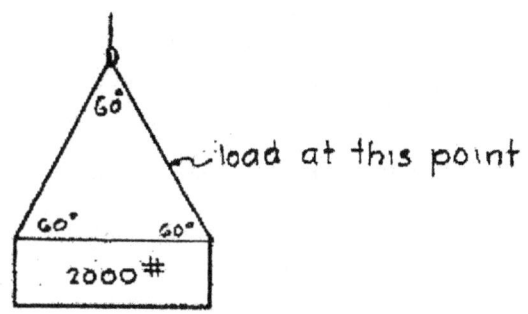

6. The load in the wire rope due to the 2000 pound weight is, in pounds, MOST NEARLY
   A. 1000
   B. 1415
   C. 1730
   D. 2000

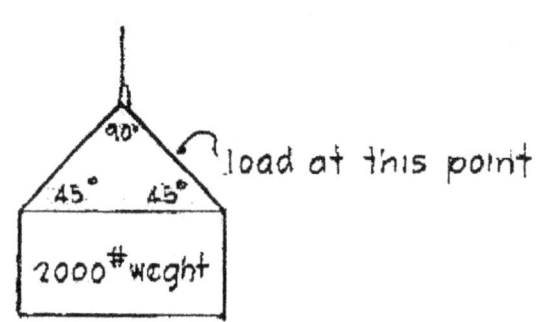

7. The minimal angle E, in degrees, that the inclined rope of the sling should make with the horizontal is
   A. 15°
   B. 20°
   C. 25°
   D. 30°

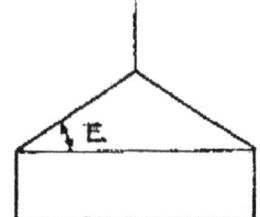

8. The load in the inclined portion of the sling in terms of W is
   A. W/2 sin E
   B. W sin E/2
   C. W/ sin E
   D. W sin E

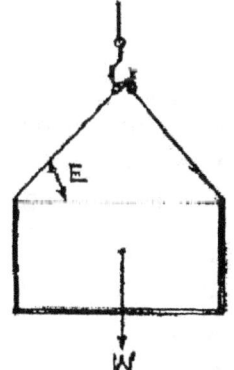

9. There are mainly two types of slings:

   A. Hook and eye, endless
   B. Eye and eye, endless
   C. Eye and eye, hook and hook
   D. Endless, hook and eye

10. For a poured socket, the metal that is poured should be

    A. lead   B. babbit   C. zinc   D. bismuth

Questions 11-12.

DIRECTIONS: Questions 11 and 12 refer to the diagram below.

The arrangement consists of a pole and cable holding a 5000 pound load. The guy ropes are for stability.

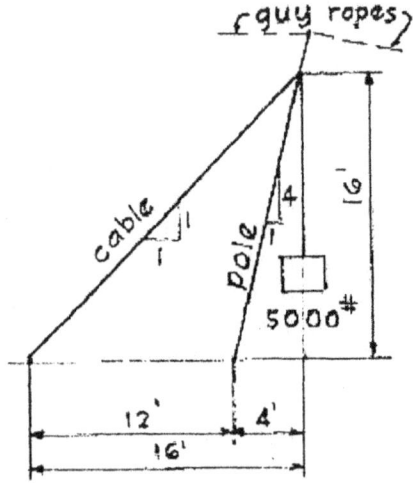

11. The load in the cable is, in pounds, MOST NEARLY

    A. 2350   B. 2400   C. 2450   D. 2500

12. The load in the pole in compression is, in pounds, MOST NEARLY

    A. 6700   B. 6750   C. 6800   D. 6850

13. A rope going over a sheave will lose 10% of the applied force due to friction. The maximum load W, in pounds, the 200 pound force at the end of the line can raise is

    A. 280
    B. 310
    C. 342
    D. 376

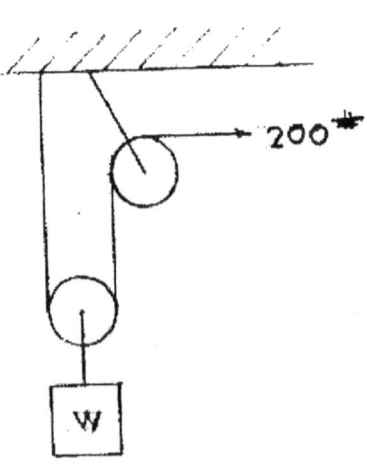

14.

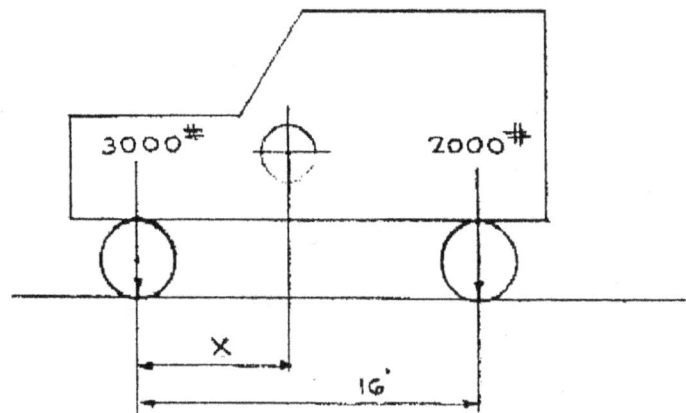

The weight of the 5000 pound car is distributed with 3000 pounds on the front tires and 2000 pounds on the rear tires. The best place to lift the car without tilting is to lift on a line a distance X feet from the front tires where X equals
  A. 6.4 B. 6.9 C. 7.4 D. 8.0

Questions 15-19.

DIRECTIONS: Questions 15 through 19 refer to the truss below.

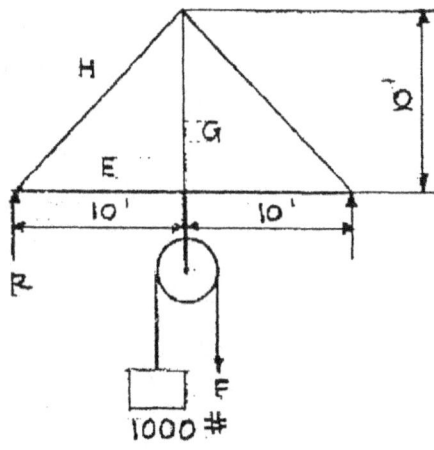

15. If the frictional resistance in the pulley is 10%, the minimum force F needed to raise the 1000# load is, in pounds, MOST NEARLY

   A. 1000   B. 1050   C. 1100   D. 1150

15.____

16. The reaction R is, in pounds, MOST NEARLY

   A. 1000   B. 1050   C. 1100   D. 1150

16.____

17. The load in member G is, in pounds, MOST NEARLY

   A. 2000   B. 2025   C. 2050   D. 2100

17.____

18. The load in member E is, in pounds, MOST NEARLY

   A. 1000   B. 1025   C. 1050   D. 1100

18.____

19. The load in member H is, in pounds, MOST NEARLY

   A. 1420   B. 1435   C. 1450   D. 1485

19.____

Questions 20-24.

DIRECTIONS: Questions 20 through 24 refer to the frame shown below.

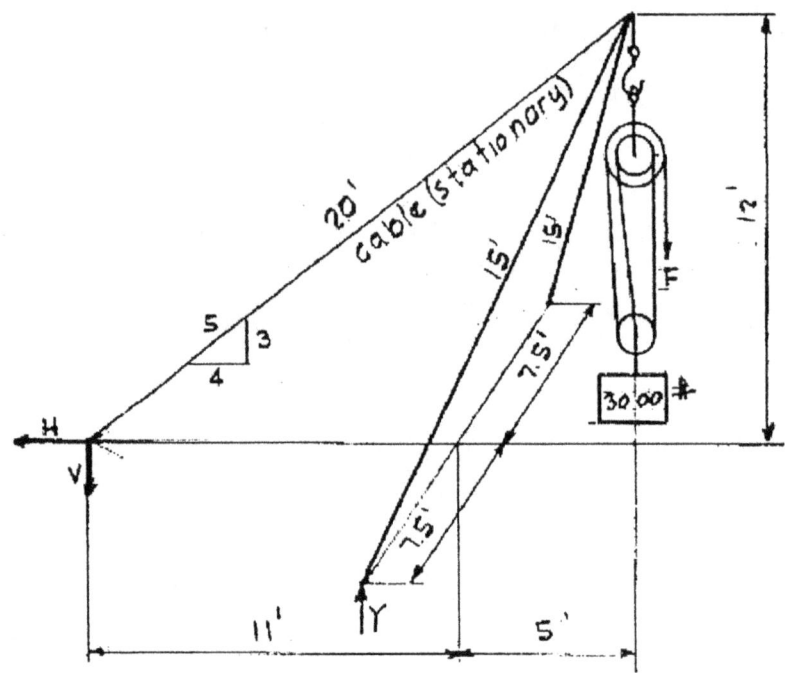

20. Neglecting friction, the minimum pulling force F needed to raise the 3000 pound load is, in pounds, MOST NEARLY

    A. 1000 B. 1250 C. 1500 D. 2000

21. The vertical component V of the force needed to hold the cable in place is, in pounds, MOST NEARLY

    A. 1250 B. 1360 C. 1680 D. 1820

22. The horizontal component H of the force needed to hold the cable in place is, in pounds, MOST NEARLY

    A. 1660 B. 1800 C. 2420 D. 2580

23. The load in the cable is, in pounds, MOST NEARLY

    A. 2075 B. 2250 C. 3025 D. 3225

24. The vertical component Y of the force needed to counteract the 15 foot member in compression is, in pounds, MOST NEARLY

    A. 2700 B. 2900 C. 3100 D. 3300

25. The mechanical advantage of this system, neglecting friction, is
    A. 6
    B. 9
    C. 12
    D. 15

KEY (CORRECT ANSWERS)

1. B
2. C
3. C
4. B
5. D

6. B
7. D
8. A
9. B
10. C

11. A
12. D
13. C
14. A
15. C

16. B
17. D
18. C
19. D
20. A

21. D
22. C
23. C
24. B
25. C

EXAMINATION SECTION
TEST 1

DIRECTIONS: Each question or incomplete statement is followed by several suggested answers or completions. Select the one that BEST answers the question or completes the statement. *PRINT THE LETTER OF THE CORRECT ANSWER IN THE SPACE AT THE RIGHT.*

1. According to OSHA regulations, a directional sign posted at a work site must have _____ as the predominant color in its upper panel and borders.

    A. yellow   B. black   C. green   D. red

2. Typically, drum anchors should be built to favor _____-lay rope.

    A. right   B. left   C. lang   D. alternate

3. A braided synthetic fiber rope with a nylon cover and nylon core has a nominal diameter of 1 1/2".
    Its approximate safe working load is _____ pounds.

    A. 4,800   B. 8,000   C. 12,800   D. 19,400

4. Which chain sling end fitting is preferred in modern rigging operations?

    A. Connecting link   B. Master ring
    C. Oblong master link   D. Pear-shaped master link

5. Bars used to secure material hoists should NOT be closer than _____ from the hoistway line.

    A. 8 inches   B. 1 foot   C. 2 feet   D. 4 feet

6. Which part of a block provides the structural means of transmitting the sheave load to the block's connections?

    A. Sheave   B. Side plates
    C. Shell   D. Center pin

7. Braided wire rope slings must have a minimum clear length AT LEAST _____ times the component rope diameter between the loop ends or fittings.

    A. 4   B. 10   C. 12   D. 40

8. What type of sheave is USUALLY used on fiber rope blocks?

    A. Plain bore   B. Bronze bushed
    C. Roller bearing   D. Antifriction

9. When the horizontal angle of a wire rope sling's legs is 45, the reduction in lifting capacity will be about _____%.

    A. 15   B. 30   C. 50   D. 70

10. What type of wire rope strand pattern uses two sizes of wire, with very small wires fitting in the spaces between the inner and outer rows of same-sized wires?

    A. Basic
    B. Warrington
    C. Filler
    D. Seale

11. OSHA regulations require that materials stored inside buildings under construction shall NOT be placed within _____ feet of any hoistway or inside floor openings.

    A. 3
    B. 6
    C. 10
    D. 15

12. The designated (manufacturer's) breaking strength of a rope, divided by its factor of safety, will give the quantity of the rope's

    A. safe working load
    B. working limit
    C. tensile strength
    D. rated capacity

13. A wire rope with a specialized 5 x 19 construction will be classified as a(n)

    A. spring lay
    B. marlin clad
    C. tiller rope
    D. flattened strand

14. The approximate weight of cast aluminum is _____ pounds per cubic foot.

    A. 165
    B. 250
    C. 330
    D. 450

15. Which type of synthetic fiber rope USUALLY will absorb no moisture?

    A. Nylon
    B. Polyester
    C. Polypropylene
    D. Polyethylene

16. Typically, what is the minimum safety factor of a wire rope used for rigging?

    A. 5
    B. 7
    C. 9
    D. 12

17. Which device should ALWAYS be used when connecting a sling leg to an eyebolt?

    A. Bail
    B. Thimble
    C. Socket
    D. Shackle

18. When using fiber rope, the minimum clear length between eye splices must be equal to _____ times the rope diameter.

    A. 4
    B. 6
    C. 10
    D. 14

19. The approximate weight of light aggregate load-bearing concrete is _____ pounds per cubic foot.

    A. 55-70
    B. 70-105
    C. 110-115
    D. 120-140

20. What should the approximate length, in inches, of seizing be for a wire rope with a diameter from 1" to 1 5/16"?

    A. 1/4
    B. 1 1/4
    C. 2 1/2
    D. 4

21. Which type of eye splice is recommended for nearly all rigging and hoisting use?

    A. Tucked
    B. Hand-spliced
    C. Fold-back
    D. Flemish

22. OSHA regulations require that a 10B fire extinguisher be placed within _____ feet of a location where more than 5 gallons of flammable or combustible solutions are being used on the jobsite.

    A. 10   B. 25   C. 50   D. 100

23. Fiber ropes should be stored at a humidity of _____%.

    A. 0-20   B. 20-40   C. 40-60   D. 60-80

24. A 1" chain, used in a double-branch sling with vertical and horizontal load angles of 45, has a rated capacity of _____ pounds.

    A. 38,750   B. 54,800   C. 67,100   D. 82,000

25. A wire rope with a nominal diameter between 1/4" and 1 1/4" will NORMALLY be used as a(n)

    A. mooring line   B. running rope
    C. elevator rope   D. guy line

KEY (CORRECT ANSWERS)

1. B	11. B
2. A	12. A
3. C	13. B
4. C	14. A
5. C	15. C
6. B	16. A
7. D	17. D
8. A	18. C
9. B	19. B
10. C	20. B

21. D
22. C
23. C
24. B
25. D

TEST 2

DIRECTIONS: Each question or incomplete statement is followed by several suggested answers or completions. Select the one that BEST answers the question or completes the statement. *PRINT THE LETTER OF THE CORRECT ANSWER IN THE SPACE AT THE RIGHT.*

1. The approximate weight of white pine lumber is _____ pounds per cubic foot.   1._____
   A. 7   B. 26   C. 67   D. 109

2. A three-end bridle sling is made from a wire rope with a diameter of 1/2". The horizontal   2._____
   angle of the sling's legs is 45.
   The sling's approximate safe working load is _____ pounds.
   A. 3,200   B. 6,000   C. 14,400   D. 36,000

3. Generally, the STRONGEST wire rope end attachment is the   3._____
   A. lead-poured socket   B. babbit
   C. master ring   D. zinc-poured socket

4. At each job site, the employer is responsible for proof-testing each lifting accessory to   4._____
   _____% of its rated load before allowing its use.
   A. 85   B. 100   C. 125   D. 150

5. The ends of two ropes, or of the same rope, are often intertwined to make a continuous   5._____
   rope.
   This is known as a
   A. hitch   B. knot   C. grommet   D. bend

6. Driveways between and around combustible storage piles shall be AT LEAST _____   6._____
   feet wide, according to OSHA regulations.
   A. 8   B. 12   C. 15   D. 20

7. 90% of all mesh slings are worked with a _____ hitch.   7._____
   A. bridle   B. vertical   C. basket   D. choker

8. Lumber stacked at a construction site shall NOT be piled higher than _____ feet,   8._____
   according to OSHA regulations.
   A. 5   B. 10   C. 15   D. 20

9. When calculating the size of bearing plate required for beam loading on a masonry wall,   9._____
   which factor will determine the plate dimension parallel to the beam length?
   A. Plate thickness   B. Wall thickness
   C. Wall surface area   D. Beam width

10. Which of the following is NOT a common type of multipart wire rope sling?   10._____
    A. Round-braided   B. Single choker
    C. Flat-braided   D. Cable-laid

11. Masonry blocks stacked at a construction site shall be stepped back one-half block per tier above the _____ foot level, according to OSHA regulations.
    A. 3   B. 6   C. 10   D. 15

12. A block loaded with a _____ will have a lower rated working load than other blocks.
    A. eye   B. ring   C. hook   D. shackle

13. Which type of synthetic fiber rope USUALLY has the greatest ability to absorb shock loading?
    A. Nylon
    B. Polyester
    C. Polypropylene
    D. Polyethylene

14. A cylindrical steel boiler is 5 feet in diameter, 8 feet long, and is made of 3/8" steel plate. The ends of the boiler are capped with 1/2" plate. A square foot of 1/8" steel plate weighs 5.1 lb.
    The weight of the boiler is _____ pounds.
    A. 800.5   B. 1,922   C. 2,722.5   D. 4,622.5

15. Synthetic web slings of polyester and nylon must NOT be used at temperatures in excess of _____ °F.
    A. 100   B. 180   C. 200   D. 280

16. What type of block is used only with fiber ropes?
    A. Tackle
    B. Utility
    C. Snatch
    D. Crane and hook

17. A manila rope with a 1" diameter is used to form a choker-hitch sling.
    The sling's rated capacity is _____ pounds.
    A. 900   B. 1,800   C. 2,600   D. 3,100

18. Which area of operation requires the lowest illumination intensity for the lighting equipment used?
    A. Loading platforms
    B. General construction areas
    C. Rigging lofts
    D. Offices

19. Materials that may create a fire hazard at an indoors job site must be segregated by a barrier that has a rated fire resistance of AT LEAST
    A. 10 minutes
    B. 30 minutes
    C. 1 hour
    D. 4 hours

20. What should always be used to secure turnbuckle fittings?
    A. Lock nuts
    B. Clamps
    C. Jam nuts
    D. Wire

21. Which type of rope splice is normally the BEST for use with sheaves and blocks?
    A. Eye   B. Long   C. Short   D. Side

22. A wire standing rope must be removed from service when there are _____ or more randomly distributed broken wires in one lay.   22._____

    A. 1   B. 3   C. 6   D. 9

23. According to OSHA regulations, a safety instruction sign posted at a work site must have _____ as the predominant color in its upper panel and borders.   23._____

    A. yellow   B. black   C. green   D. red

24. Typically, what is the minimum safety factor of a wire rope used with a crane?   24._____

    A. 4   B. 6   C. 8   D. 10

25. If a fiber rope's internal yarns remain unbroken, repeated loading of the rope will   25._____

    A. increase the rope's breaking strength
    B. not stretch the core fibers during loading
    C. increase the rope's elasticity
    D. decrease the rope's breaking strength

KEY (CORRECT ANSWERS)

1. B	11. B
2. B	12. C
3. D	13. A
4. C	14. C
5. D	15. B
6. C	16. A
7. D	17. A
8. D	18. A
9. B	19. C
10. B	20. D

21. B
22. B
23. C
24. B
25. A

EXAMINATION SECTION
TEST 1

DIRECTIONS: Each question or incomplete statement is followed by several suggested answers or completions. Select the one that BEST answers the question or completes the statement. *PRINT THE LETTER OF THE CORRECT ANSWER IN THE SPACE AT THE RIGHT.*

1. The proper operation and maintenance of any crane, shovel, or dragline is CHIEFLY the responsibility of the   1.____

    A. foreman   B. oiler   C. mechanic   D. operator

2. The *angle indicator* on a power-operated crane measures the   2.____

    A. angle of the boom to the horizontal
    B. angle of the boom to the vertical
    C. tilt of the housing which covers the rotating operator's station
    D. angle between the boom and the whipline

3. On a power-operated crane, the device used to prevent the boom from being pulled over the top of the cab is the   3.____

    A. brake   B. boom stop
    C. boom point   D. base

4. The block and sheave arrangement on the boom point to which the topping lift cable is reeved for lowering and raising the boom is called the   4.____

    A. boom harness   B. cableway
    C. axle   D. bogie

5. The extension attached to the boom point of a crane to provide added length for lifting is known as a   5.____

    A. folding boom   B. lay
    C. mast   D. jib

6. The *Load Rating Chart* of a mobile crane makes no allowance for   6.____

    A. range of crane load ratings
    B. operating radii and boom angles
    C. permissible boom lengths
    D. operating speeds

7. The WEAKEST part of any crane hoist or sling should be the   7.____

    A. clip   B. link   C. hook   D. clamp

8. Of the following types of equipment, the one which is MOST often used for excavation operations where extended reach (40 to 60 feet) is an important factor is the   8.____

    A. pay loader   B. power shovel
    C. dragline   D. backhoe

9. Assume that a man is reeling wire onto a smooth-faced drum. With the man facing the drum, the wire is going from the man over the top of the drum, starting with that part of the drum at the man's right side.
   The procedure being followed by this man is

   A. *correct* as described
   B. *wrong* because the wire should be reeled under the drum
   C. *wrong* because the reeling should start at the man's left side
   D. *wrong* because wire should not be reeled onto a smoothfaced drum

10. The point at which vibration will cause the GREATEST weakness in a wire rope used on rapid hoisting rigs is, approximately, _____ to _____ feet above the load attachment.

    A. 5; 20   B. 30; 45   C. 50; 65   D. 70; 85

11. The efficiency of a clipped attachment depends on the manner in which the clips are put on the wire rope, the tightness of nuts on the clips, *and* the _____ the wire rope.

    A. diameter of   B. construction of
    C. number of clips used on   D. manufacturer of

12. Of the following types of end connections, the one which is NOT generally used for attaching a wire rope to a clamshell bucket is the

    A. socket attachment   B. spliced eye attachment
    C. clipped attachment   D. wedge socket

13. A Langlay wire rope should be used ONLY with a load that

    A. is relatively light
    B. cannot rotate as it is being lifted
    C. is supported on a float
    D. will keep the rope tight

14. Of the following materials, the one MOST commonly used to make crane brake linings is

    A. cotton fabric   B. bakelite
    C. neoprene   D. asbestos fabric

15. The MAIN reason why an operator of a diesel-powered rig must not permit the diesel engine to run out of fuel is to prevent

    A. condensation in the fuel tank
    B. damage to the fuel injection system
    C. an increase in coolant temperature
    D. damage to the oil pressure regulating valve

16. If a power shovel, equipped with an electric power plant that has a single electric motor drive, is operating sluggishly due to lack of power, it would be BEST to check the motor with a

    A. tachometer and a rheostat
    B. dwell meter
    C. voltmeter and an ammeter
    D. Bailey meter

17. An operator of a gasoline-powered rig permits the engine to idle unnecessarily for long periods of time. Of the following, the MOST probable result of this practice is that the

    A. rig will operate more smoothly
    B. lubricating oil will be diluted
    C. radiator water temperature will rise too high
    D. clutch controls will freeze

18. Before fully engaging the engine clutch to set a piece of machinery in operation, the operator should

    A. partially engage and then disengage the engine clutch to test its operation
    B. check the operating controls to be sure that the clutches are in neutral
    C. examine the gears for proper lubrication
    D. examine the main machinery, making certain that no obstruction prevents its normal operation

19. An operator of a crane wished to change over from dragline operation to a clamshell operation.
    Assuming there is no boom change, the minimum amount of time it would take three men to make the conversion would be, MOST NEARLY, in the range of _____ to _____ hours.

    A. 2; 3   B. 6; 7   C. 8; 9   D. 10; 11

20. The PRIMARY function of outrigging on a truck crane is to

    A. extend the boom length
    B. avoid wear of the hoist wire rope
    C. give side support to the truck body
    D. strengthen the structural members of the boom

21. The lowering of a load by a direct-current-powered crane is controlled by _____ braking.

    A. hydraulic   B. mechanical
    C. dynamic   D. double disc

22. The shaft which operates the valves of a gasoline engine is the _____ shaft.

    A. crank   B. distributor
    C. valve   D. cam

23. Of the following, the BEST practical way to prevent a lead plate storage battery from freezing in cold weather is to

    A. turn off all the auxiliaries when not in use
    B. keep the specific gravity of the electrolyte below 1.150
    C. keep it well charged
    D. disconnect the battery cables when the machine is not in use

24. Grades in excavation work are usually designated by

    A. degree   B. percent   C. height   D. elevation

25. Of the following, the one that is a positive mechanical device for engaging or disengaging power is the

    A. universal
    B. clutch
    C. brake
    D. unloader

26. Of the following, the tool or device that is commonly used to check the firing of spark plugs in a gasoline engine is a(n)

    A. tachometer
    B. ammeter
    C. screw driver with an insulated handle
    D. feeler gauge

27. If the power fails when hoisting a load, the FIRST thing an operator should do is to

    A. land the load under brake control
    B. communicate with the appointed individual in charge of operations
    C. move all clutch or other power controls to the *off* position
    D. set all brakes and locking devices

28. In a 4-stroke-cycle, full-diesel engine, the fuel is ignited by

    A. a jump spark
    B. special spark plugs
    C. highly compressed air
    D. hot exhaust gases

29. The function of the pre-combustion chamber on a diesel engine is to

    A. eliminate pre-ignition
    B. obtain higher compression pressures
    C. pre-cool the lubricating oil
    D. assure complete combustion of the fuel

30. The PRIMARY reason for including a thermal overload device in an electrical circuit containing a 40-horsepower A.C. motor is to

    A. increase the motor's efficiency
    B. control the speed of the motor
    C. protect the motor from overheating
    D. decrease the torque of the motor

31. The MAIN function of the intercooler in a two-stage air compressor is to

    A. cool the lubricating oil
    B. cool the air between stages of compression
    C. permit the expansion of combustion products
    D. remove impurities from the air

32. The relief valve on a gasoline-powered portable air compressor is located on the

    A. oil reserve tank
    B. suction side of the air compressor
    C. discharge side of the air compressor
    D. combustion exhaust manifold

33. In a diesel engine, the injection pump and the nozzle are lubricated by

   A. an SAE 30 oil
   B. the diesel fuel itself
   C. heat-resistant grease
   D. mineral oil

34. The SAE number is an index of a diesel lubricating oil's

   A. specific gravity
   B. film strength
   C. viscosity
   D. anti-foaming ability

35. Excessive lubrication of diesel cylinders may cause

   A. condensation in the cylinders
   B. dangerous vapors in the cylinders
   C. pre-ignition in the cylinders
   D. sticking piston rings

36. The method by which water generally enters the lubricating oil system of a diesel engine is through

   A. rain dripping down into the vents
   B. condensation of the combustion products
   C. a leaky crankcase cover
   D. radiator spill-over

37. In an operator's manual, a lubricant is designated as SUMMER SAE-140 E.P. This lubricant would MOST probably be

   A. an easy-pour lubricant
   B. a grease
   C. an extreme-pressure lubricant
   D. interchangeable with chassis grease

38. A sudden change in the color of a lubricating oil in an operating engine would MOST probably be caused by a(n)

   A. dirty filter
   B. clogged oil breather
   C. overfill of lubricating oil
   D. severe overload and heat

39. The air cleaner of an air compressor is of the oil bath type.
    Of the following substances, the one that it is BEST to use to clean the filter element of this cleaner is

   A. gasoline
   B. oil
   C. water spray
   D. wood alcohol

40. The shipper shaft of a shovel boom is generally located close to the boom's

   A. mid-point
   B. top
   C. bottom
   D. drum

KEY (CORRECT ANSWERS)

1. D	11. C	21. C	31. B
2. A	12. A	22. D	32. C
3. B	13. B	23. C	33. B
4. A	14. D	24. B	34. C
5. D	15. B	25. B	35. D
6. D	16. C	26. C	36. B
7. C	17. B	27. D	37. C
8. C	18. D	28. C	38. D
9. A	19. A	29. D	39. B
10. A	20. C	30. C	40. A

TEST 2

DIRECTIONS: Each question or incomplete statement is followed by several suggested answers or completions. Select the one that BEST answers the question or completes the statement. *PRINT THE LETTER OF THE CORRECT ANSWER IN THE SPACE AT THE RIGHT.*

1. A friction-type clutch is preferable to a positive-type clutch in crane applications because a   1.____

   A. positive clutch can be applied only at high speeds
   B. friction clutch needs no maintenance
   C. positive clutch cannot take loads as well as a friction clutch
   D. friction clutch can be engaged at any speed

2. Of the following types of pumps, the one which is NOT generally found on power-driven mobile machinery is the _____ pump.   2.____

   A. piston-type rotary B. reciprocating type
   C. gear-type D. balanced vane-type

3. The term *CFM*, as applied to the capacity of air compressors, is an abbreviation for   3.____

   A. compressor feed mechanism
   B. centrifugal force meter
   C. compression fuel machine
   D. cubic feet per minute

4. In a certain crane, a horizontal roller chain drive provides power to the jack shaft. In order that there be proper tension in the roller chain, the chain should be adjusted so that there is   4.____

   A. no sag
   B. a small amount of sag
   C. sufficient sag to allow the chain to droop at its midpoint to the level of the center line of the driving sprocket
   D. sufficient sag so that the top chain and the bottom chain will make an angle of 60° at the driving sprocket

5. Of the following, a switch operated by the motion of a moving part of an electrically powered machine is usually called a _____ switch.   5.____

   A. disconnect B. remote-control
   C. limit D. service

6. The BEST type of torch to use for cutting wire rope used on a land-based construction site is the   6.____

   A. oxy-acetylene torch B. oxy-hydrogen lance
   C. air-propane torch D. oxy-butane torch

7. Of the following gear types, the one that would NOT be used to transmit power between two parallel shafts is the _____ gear.   7.____

   A. spur B. herringbone
   C. helical D. bevel

8. The cylinder of a 2-stroke-cycle diesel engine is scavenged by the

   A. mixture of fuel oil and exhaust gases
   B. mixture of fuel oil and intake air
   C. intake fuel
   D. combustion air

9. A COMMON cause of engine back pressure in a gasoline engine is a

   A. rusted muffler   B. blocked muffler passage
   C. loose exhaust pipe   D. corroded muffler bracket

10. A grease with a consistency number of 2 is classified as

    A. semifluid   B. hard   C. very hard   D. medium

11. The one of the following to which a micron rating would be assigned is a(n)

    A. grease   B. oil filter
    C. strainer   D. magnetic plug

12. An oil is rated as SAE 20W.
    The number *20* refers to the oil's

    A. viscosity at 0° F   B. detergent factor
    C. specific volume   D. rate of deterioration

13. Crane machinery and equipment is BEST lubricated

    A. whenever it is needed
    B. when severe vibration occurs
    C. when out of service
    D. at scheduled times

14. Of the following parts of an electric motor, the one which should be checked for proper lubrication is the

    A. bearings   B. commutator
    C. rotating field   D. windings

15. Of the following liquids, the one which is used as an electrolyte in a lead-plate storage battery is

    A. hydrochloric acid   B. salt water
    C. sulphuric acid   D. ammonia water

16. A battery hydrometer is used mainly to determine a battery's

    A. specific gravity   B. temperature
    C. resistance   D. salinity

17. The BEST method to use to remove a stuck gear from a shaft is to

    A. use a wheel puller
    B. use heavy hammer blows to loosen the gear
    C. heat the shaft and then remove the gear
    D. apply oil and rotate the gear slowly

18. Internal leakage in the hydraulic oil line piping system of a mobile unit will

    A. provide lubrication for such parts as shafts and pistons
    B. result in an oil loss from the lubrication system
    C. not cause a power loss
    D. decrease with normal wear of the parts of the unit

19. A preventive maintenance program is a program in which

    A. machinery is serviced whenever required
    B. maintenance of machinery is performed on a regular schedule
    C. the machines are maintained in such a way that there is never any down-time
    D. inspection of machinery is performed only during slack periods

20. An external gear pump consists essentially of

    A. two meshed gears in a closely fitted housing
    B. one gear which is activated by the moving fluid
    C. a piston turning a gear in an enclosed housing
    D. an inlet and outlet reciprocating valve

21. The MINIMUM width of each seizing that is wrapped around a wirerope that is to be cut should be _____ the diameter of the rope.

    A. equal to   B. 1 1/2 times
    C. 2 times   D. 3 times

22. Before cutting a 1" diameter non-preformed regular-lay 6x19 wire rope, the MINIMUM number of seizings that should be placed on each side of the spot where the wire rope is to be cut is

    A. 1   B. 2   C. 3   D. 4

23. When seizing a wire rope, a *seizing iron* is mainly used to

    A. measure the length of seizing wire
    B. straighten the seizing wire
    C. loosen a badly made seizing
    D. wrap the seizing tightly

24. Of the following materials, the one from which seizing wire is made is

    A. copper   B. annealed iron
    C. nylon   D. aluminum

25. Oil used on wire rope which goes through the sheaves and over the drum of a crane will generally

    A. cause the drum to slip
    B. increase the life of the rope
    C. gum up the sheaves
    D. cause the wire to have a slimy surface

26. As a result of insertion of a steel thimble into a spliced eye attachment of a wire rope, the

    A. load will be equally distributed to the wire rope
    B. wire rope will flatten out of shape
    C. wire strands of the rope will tend to break when load is applied
    D. holding power of the attachment will be increased

27. Wedge sockets are MOST frequently used to

    A. temporarily attach wire rope to a piece of equipment
    B. make permanent attachments of wire rope to a piece of equipment
    C. connect two different sizes of wire rope to each other
    D. adjust the length of wire rope to fit the job

28. A *left-lay, regular-lay* wire rope has

    A. the wires laid right-handed and the strands left-handed
    B. the wires laid left-handed and the strands right-handed
    C. both wires and strands laid right-handed
    D. both wires and strands laid left-handed

Questions 29 - 33.

DIRECTIONS: Questions 29 through 33 inclusive are to be answered in accordance with the following paragraphs.

Exhaust valve clearance adjustment on diesel engines is very important for proper operation of the engine. Insufficient clearance between the exhaust valve stem and the rocker arm causes a loss of compression and, after a while, burning of the valves and valve seat inserts. On the other hand, too much valve clearance will result in noisy operation of the engine.

Exhaust valves that are maintained in good operating condition will result in efficient combustion in the engine. Valve seats must be true and unpitted and valve stems must work smoothly within the valve guides. Long valve life will result from proper maintenance and operation of the engine.

Engine operating temperatures should be maintained between 160° F and 185° F. Low operating temperatures result in incomplete combustion and the deposit of fuel lacquers on valves.

29. According to the above paragraphs, too much valve clearance will cause the engine to operate

    A. slowly   B. noisily   C. smoothly   D. cold

30. On the basis of the information given in the above paragraphs, operating temperatures of a diesel engine should be between _____ F and _____ F.

    A. 125°; 130°   B. 140°; 150°
    C. 160°; 185°   D. 190°; 205°

31. According to the above paragraphs, the deposit of fuel lacquers on valves is caused by

    A. high operating temperatures
    B. insufficient valve clearance
    C. low operating temperatures
    D. efficient combustion

32. According to the above paragraphs, for efficient operation of the engine, valve seats must

    A. have sufficient clearance
    B. be true and unpitted
    C. operate at low temperatures
    D. be adjusted regularly

33. According to the above paragraphs, a loss of compression is due to insufficient clearance between the exhaust valve stem and the

    A. rocker arm   B. valve seat
    C. valve seat inserts   D. valve guides

34. The BEST of the following ways to deal with a helper assigned to you who is a chronic complainer is to

    A. tell him to stop complaining so much
    B. treat each complaint as if it were valid
    C. walk away from him when he starts to complain
    D. tell him his complaints are senseless

35. An oiler assigned to service your crane has always performed his duties diligently, but for the past several weeks he has been lax.
    Of the following actions, the BEST one to take would be to

    A. recommend his transfer
    B. report him to your superior
    C. re-assign him to office work
    D. ask him if there is anything wrong

36. Of the following, the BEST procedure for an operator to follow when breaking in a new oiler on the job is to

    A. assign work that he is capable of performing
    B. give him minor work assignments to do until he proves he is capable of doing the job
    C. praise him even though his work is not satisfactory
    D. criticize the man in a loud manner when he makes an error

37. An operator of a crane working a short distance from where you are operating, is rendered unconscious when the boom of his crane hits an electric power line.
    Of the following, after safely securing your machine, the FIRST procedure for you to follow would be to

    A. immediately apply artificial respiration to the unconscious operator
    B. call a physician
    C. determine if an electrical hazard still exists aboard the crane
    D. administer a stimulant to the unconscious operator

38. A crane engineman is operating a gasoline-powered crane and sees smoke coming from the engine.
    In this situation, the operator should FIRST

    A. call his helper for assistance
    B. get the fire extinguisher
    C. shut the engine off
    D. wait for flames to appear

39. Assume that a helper has fallen off the crane and is unable to move.
    The BEST procedure to follow in this instance would be to

    A. seek medical aid, letting him lie where he is
    B. place him in a sitting position
    C. give him a stimulant to drink
    D. call the other workers to remove him from the work site

40. Of the following types of fire extinguishing agents, the one that should NOT be used on an oil fire in an oil storage area is

    A. foam
    B. dry chemical
    C. carbon dioxide
    D. soda acid

KEY (CORRECT ANSWERS)

1. D	11. B	21. A	31. C
2. B	12. A	22. C	32. B
3. D	13. D	23. D	33. A
4. B	14. A	24. B	34. B
5. C	15. C	25. B	35. D
6. A	16. A	26. D	36. A
7. D	17. A	27. A	37. C
8. D	18. A	28. A	38. C
9. B	19. B	29. B	39. A
10. D	20. A	30. C	40. D

EXAMINATION SECTION
TEST 1

DIRECTIONS: Each question or incomplete statement is followed by several suggested answers or completions. Select the one that BEST answers the question or completes the statement. *PRINT THE LETTER OF THE CORRECT ANSWER IN THE SPACE AT THE RIGHT.*

1. The type of crane that requires surface rail tracks is a
   A. stiff leg derrick
   B. gantry crane
   C. rotary crane
   D. jub crane

    1.____

2. Dynamic breaking is

   A. the term used when actuating a trustor brake
   B. a term used when energizing a magnetic type break
   C. closing a magnetic contactor which permits the brake to close
   D. a method of reducing the speed of some hoisting motors when lowering a load

    2.____

3. Minimum tread diameter for a 6x7 steel wire rope should be *approximately* _____ times the rope diameter.
   A. 20	B. 24	C. 36	D. 42

    3.____

4. The type of D.C. *motor most commonly* used for powering cranes is the
   A. shunt wound motor
   B. compound motor
   C. series wound motor
   D. cumulative compound motor

    4.____

5. Two similar $\frac{1}{2}$"-6-strand wire ropes are to be spliced together. If the two ropes are to be spliced by a standard short splice, the seizings should be placed _____ feet from the ends.
   A. 2	B. 5	C. 10	D. 15

    5.____

6. The type of A.C. motor *most commonly* used for powering cranes is the

   A. slip-ring type induction motor
   B. synchronous motor
   C. squirrel-cagetype, induction motor
   D. universal motor

    6.____

7. A square foot of sheet steel 3/8" thick weighs 15.3 lbs.
   A pile of sheet steel consists of 10 sheets, each measuring 4' x 8' x 3/8". This pile weighs approximately _____ ton(s).
   A. 1	B. 1.5	C. 2	D. 2.5

    7.____

8. On A.C. cranes equipped with reverse torque control on the hoist, as in magnet or bucket handling cranes, the motor brake must slow down the motor from about _____ % synch. speed to stand still and then hold the load.
   A. 35	B. 60	C. 20	D. 100

    8.____

2 (#1)

9. The wire rope which you are to use has a minimum safety factor of 5 and a breaking strength of 10,000 lbs. The maximum load in tons which you would hoist when complying with the above given data is approximately _____ ton(s).

   A. 1 B. 2 C. 3 D. 5

9.___

10. On direct current controllers where it is necessary to remove or replace blow out coils, it is very important to

   A. insert the blow out coils to give the proper polarity
   B. cross their leads before connecting them
   C. see that they are wound non-inductive
   D. see that they are not wound non-inductive

10.___

11. The blackwall hitch is used

   A. when making a temporary fastening to a hook
   B. to shorten a line
   C. for fastening a rope around a beam
   D. for towing cars

11.___

12. Worn pins and bushings in motor solenoid brakes

   A. will decrease the operating solenoid stroke
   B. will increase the operating solenoid stroke
   C. must be lubricated with graphite
   D. should not be lubricated

12.___

13. The metal used for socketing wire ropes is

   A. tin
   B. lead
   C. aluminum of the highest commercial purity
   D. zinc

13.___

14. To reverse the direction of rotation of a series-wound D.C. motor

   A. reverse both the field and the armature
   B. interchange the armature leads at the motor terminals
   C. rotate the brushes counterclockwise
   D. interchange the lines wires

14.___

15. The speed regulation of an A.C. wound rotor induction motor is best obtained by

   A. changing the stator voltage
   B. rotating the brushes on slip rings
   C. varying the resistance in the rotor circuit
   D. using a diverter

15.___

16. With the exception of slings with bridge sockets or open sockets, the length of different types of slings is taken

   A. from bearing to bearing
   B. from bearing to bearing times $\frac{1}{2}$

16.___

C. from bearing to bearing times 3/4
D. from bearing to bearing times 2

17. The size of the fuse to be used in a circuit depends upon the

   A. size of wire
   B. connected load
   C. voltage of the line
   D. rating of the switch

18. The type of lubricant commonly used for a bridge motor gear case at low temperature (below 32 degrees F) is

   A. S.A.E. 160
   B. S.A.E. 90
   C. S.A.E. 250
   D. dip-gear grease

19. When an operator of an electrically powered crane leaves the car, he *must*

   A. place all controllers in the off position
   B. place all controllers in the off position and pull the main switch
   C. test all the fuses
   D. test all the controllers

20. Variation in the size of driver wheels will cause a bridge crane to operate out of square on the runway with resulting flange wear against the side of the rail. To avoid this condition, it is necessary to keep the driver wheels paired or matched in size.
    As a general rule on cranes, the wheels should be replaced or refinished if the variation in these wheels reaches

   A. 1/16"   B. 1/8"   C. 5/16"   D. 1/4"

21. A D.C. contactor coil has one or two turns short circuited. If the coil is kept in operation

   A. it will immediately burn out
   B. it cannot burn out due only to two shorted turns
   C. it may start to hum excessively
   D. the inducted voltage in shorted turns would cause a large current to circulate and burn out the entire cell

22. If the crane is subject to constant overloading and has been in heavy duty service for a period of ten years, the load-hook should be

   A. annealed and placed back in service
   B. scrapped
   C. tempered and placed back in service
   D. continued in use for another 10 years

23. It is NOT advisable for safety to overload bridge cranes more than _____ % of rated load.

   A. 100   B. 50   C. 25   D. 10

24. In response to a sound or audible signal system the crane engineman shall lower the load when the signal sounded is _____ bells.

   A. 2   B. 3   C. 5   D. 4

25. Thermal overload protective devices for motors protect the motors against

   A. a short
   B. overload at starting
   C. temporary overloads
   D. sustained overloads

26. If the angle between the boom and the mast is decreased, the load that can be raised

   A. can be increased
   B. cannot be increased
   C. must be decreased by 10%
   D. must be decreased by 20%

27. For best results, new brushes may be fitted to commutators of D.C. machines or slip rings of A.C. machines by using

   A. sandpaper #00
   B. emery cloth
   C. a fine file
   D. sand stone

28. If a crane has a capacity of 27,500 pounds at 25 foot radius, then the load that can be raised at 40 foot radius is

   A. 50,000 pounds
   B. 27,500 pounds
   C. greater than 27,500 pounds
   D. smaller than 27,500 pounds

29. The *primary* purpose of oil in an oil-type circuit breaker is to

   A. lubricate the contents
   B. cool the breaker
   C. limit the load on the breaker
   D. quench the arc

30. A much used crane with bearings of the sleeve type should receive attention at least

   A. daily   B. weekly   C. monthly   D. yearly

31. A dash pot arrangement on a circuit breaker or motor starter provides for

   A. short-circuit protection
   B. under voltage protection
   C. delayed- time action
   D. absorbing mechanical stresses or vibration when the device is closed

32. A greatly worked crane with bearings of the ball or roller type should NOT require bearing inspection more than

   A. semi-annually
   B. weekly
   C. monthly
   D. yearly

33. Limit switches when used in connection with the operation of a hoist, serve the purpose of

   A. limiting the speed of the hoist
   B. stopping the hoist when the hoist motor controller is forced beyond a limiting point of acceleration

C. preventing the operator from raising the load above certain limits
D. preventing the operator from lowering the load

34. Crane bumpers should be

    A. fastened to the rail
    B. fastened to the girder
    C. at least 1/4 the diameter of the truck wheel in height
    D. at least 1/3 the diameter of the truck wheel in height

35. Ordinary "ring-fire," a type of sparking wholly or partially encircling the circumference of the commutator and reddish in color, is a condition *usually* brought about by

    A. incorrect brush pressure   B. open armature coil
    C. dirty commutator   D. shorted field coil

36. Bridge crane hoisting brakes should be able to carry

    A. double the rated load   B. 3 times the rated load
    C. 4 times the rated load   D. the rated load

37. Magnetic contactor tips are properly adjusted when they

    A. have a wiping or rolling motion in closing and opening
    B. make full face contact in closing and opening
    C. make line contact at the center of the face in opening and closing
    D. make line contact at top and bottom of the face in closing and opening

38. The rails of electric overhead traveling cranes should be of the correct span center throughout their entire length, with both rails level and at the same elevation. An accepted installation should have a center-to-center rail measurement deviation NOT greater than *approximately*

    A. 1 inch   B. two inches   C. 3/4 inch   D. 1/8 inch

39. The object of a rotar rheostat is to

    A. start a squirrel cage induction motor
    B. control the A.C. current of a synchronous motor
    C. start or control the speed of a wound rotor induction motor
    D. control the speed of a squirrel cage motor

40. In ordering fuses, it is necessary to specify

    A. the current capacity
    B. the voltage of the circuit
    C. current and voltage capacity
    D. voltage and length of fuse

41. Fires occurring in and around electrical apparatus are BEST extinguished by applying

    A. water
    B. sand

C. soda acid chemical solution
D. carbon dioxide or carbon tetrachloride

42. When two or more unequal resistances are connected in parallel, the equivalent or resulting resistance is

   A. *greater* than the largest resistance
   B. *smaller* than the smallest resistance
   C. *greater* than the smallest resistance
   D. *equal to* the sum of all the resistances

43. The magnetic contactors for changing direction of the rotation of motors should be

   A. electrically interlocked
   B. mechanically and electrically interlocked
   C. mechanically interlocked
   D. independently operated

44. On a crane, a squeaking noise *usually* means

   A. excessive wear on bearings and/or gear teeth
   B. a dry bearing surface
   C. a rough or dirty commutator
   D. solenoid brakes are out of adjustment

45. Energy consumption, whether A.C. or D.C. is usually measured by means of a

   A. wattmeter   B. kilowatt meter
   C. watthour meter   D. demand meter

46. A two-leg bridle sling with hooks and $\frac{1}{2}$ inch diameter ropes, has a safe load capacity of 3.2 tons with vertical legs.
When the legs are set at 90 degrees to each other, the safe load in tons is about

   A. 3.2   B. 2.2   C. 1.2   D. 1

47. Periodical inspection should be made of secondary grid resistor connections to see that they are tight and properly made.
A loosely stacked resistor will *most likely* cause

   A. burning, pitting and a change in resistance
   B. a greater inrush of current
   C. a decrease in current
   D. burning, pitting, and the resistance value will not change

48. The speed of a crane trolley motor is 900 r.p.m. If the motor pinion has 20 teeth and the gear has 80 teeth, the speed of the gear shaft is *most nearly* _____ r.p.m.

   A. 3600   B. 425   C. 325   D. 225

49. An electrical conductor has 19 strands, and the diameter of each strand is 114.7 mils. The size of the conductor in C.M. is about

   A. 400,000   B. 350,000   C. 300,000   D. 250,000

50. The field of a series motor should be

   A. of sufficient cross-section to carry the rated armature current
   B. connected in parallel with the armature
   C. connected across the line
   D. in series with a diver

51. A current transformer has a ratio of 20 to 1. When the ammeter connected to the transformer secondary reads 3.3 amps., the primary current is _____ amps.

   A. 11   B. 33   C. 66   D. 99

52. During manufacture of wire rope the hemp center and strands; are thoroughly impregnated with

   A. lubricant
   B. red lead
   C. clear varnish
   D. shellac

53. A device which may be used to ascertain whether an electric wiring system is energized with direct or alternating current is(are)

   A. test lamps in multiple
   B. test lamps in series
   C. a neon tester
   D. a megger

54. The characteristics of the series motor which makes its use desirable, is that a large increase in torque is obtained

   A. with a large increase in voltage
   B. with a moderate increase in current
   C. when lowering a load
   D. with a moderate decrease in current

55. To reverse the direction of rotation of a 3-phase inductions motor

   A. the three line leads are interchanged
   B. the secondary grid leads are interchanged
   C. any two line leads are interchanged
   D. only two secondary grid leads are interchanged

56. The bearings of a wound-rotor induction motor are hot, but not hotter than the other parts of the motor.
   This condition would *most likely* be caused by

   A. dirty oil in the bearings
   B. a short-circuited rotor coil
   C. an overload on the motor
   D. the rings in the bearings not rotating

57. Overload protective units of the time-limit type in circuit breakers or controllers which are used as running protection for motors should be set at NOT more than

   A. 125% of the motor full load current
   B. the maximum starting current of the motor
   C. the current carrying capacity of the wires
   D. 110% of the full load current of the motor

58. In seizing wire rope, the seizing strand should be wound around rope at LEAST _____ times, keeping wraps close together and in tension.

    A. 6   B. 7   C. 9   D. 11

59. The wires of 3-phase 208v circuit carrying 800 amps should be protected by

    A. cartridge fuses with knife blade contact
    B. a circuit breaker
    C. thermo cut-outs
    D. a cut-out switch

60. For safety, the *minimum* number of U-type clips which should be used for securing a $\frac{1}{2}"$ wire rope around a thimble is

    A. 3   B. 5   C. 2   D. 4

KEY (CORRECT ANSWERS)

1.	B	16.	A	31.	C	46.	B
2.	D	17.	A	32.	B	47.	A
3.	D	18.	B	33.	C	48.	D
4.	C	19.	B	34.	B	49.	D
5.	C	20.	B	35.	B	50.	A
6.	A	21.	B	36.	A	51.	C
7.	D	22.	A	37.	A	52.	A
8.	A	23.	C	38.	D	53.	C
9.	A	24.	B	39.	C	54.	B
10.	A	25.	D	40.	C	55.	C
11.	A	26.	A	41.	D	56.	C
12.	B	27.	A	42.	B	57.	A
13.	D	28.	D	43.	B	58.	B
14.	B	29.	D	44.	B	59.	B
15.	C	30.	A	45.	C	60.	D

EXAMINATION SECTION
TEST 1

DIRECTIONS: Each question or incomplete statement is followed by several suggested answers or completions. Select the one that BEST answers the question or completes the statement. *PRINT THE LETTER OF THE CORRECT ANSWER IN THE SPACE AT THE RIGHT.*

Questions 1-10.

DIRECTIONS: Questions 1 through 10 are to be answered SOLELY on the basis of the information in the following passage from a section of the electrical code.

CRANES AND HOISTS

Section B30-158.0 Wires
           B30-159.0 Installation of Wires
           B30-160.0 Collector Conductors
           B30-161.0 Collectors.
           B30-162.0 Switches and cutouts.
           B30-163.0 Controllers
           B30-164.0 Grounding
           B30-174.0 Hazardous Locations

Section B30-158.0 - Wires.
    a. Wiring other than bare collector wires shall be rubber covered, slow-burning type (S.B.), or asbestos covered (type A).
    b. Rubber covered wire shall not be smaller than No. 12, except on pilot circuits of controllers, where No. 14 may be used.
    c. Slow-burning (type S.B.) wire shall be used where exposed to external heat in excess of 167° F. (75° C.) and asbestos covered wire (type A) where the temperature exceeds 194° F. (90° C.) between resistances and contact plates, unless exposed to moisture, when rubber covered wires shall be used. When rubber covered wires so used are bunched, outer covering of each conductor shall be flame-retarding or shall be taped with a flameproof covering. (As amended by Local Law No. 28.)

Section B30-159.0 - Installation of Wires.
    a. Wiring other than bare collector wires and necessary short lengths of open wires at resistors and collectors shall be installed in rigid conduit or electrical metallic tubing, except that necessary sections of armored cable or flexible metallic conduit may be employed for connection to motors, electric brake, or other features which must be in movable relation to the conduit or tubing system and provided further that in dry places where space is limited, each wire may be separately encased in flexible tubing securely fastened in place.
    b. Collector wires shall not be used as feeders for any equipment other than the crane or cranes which they are primarily designed to serve.
    c. Where wires of cranes and hoist circuits leave conduit or other metal raceways, they shall be individually bushed, except that more than four wires may be bunched, taped with a flameproof covering, and bushed with an insulating bushing. The metal raceway shall terminate as close to the wire terminals as convenience in handling will permit.

d. The primary and secondary circuits for alternating current motors and direct current motor conduits shall be run as complete individual circuits for each motor on the crane. The use of common return wires for two or more motors shall not be permitted.

Section B30-160.0 - Collector Conductors.

a. When wires are used as conductors, they shall be secured at the ends by means of strain insulators and shall be so mounted on approved insulators that the extreme limit of displacement of the wire will not bring the latter within less than one and one-half inches from the surface wired over.

b. Main collector wires carried along runways shall be supported on insulating supports placed at intervals not exceeding twenty feet. When run on the same horizontal plane, such wires shall be separated not less than 6 inches, except for monorail hoists, where a spacing of not less than three inches may be used; when run otherwise, the spacing shall not be less than eight inches. Where necessary, intervals between insulating supports may be increased to 40 feet, the separation between wires being increased proportionally.

c. Bridge collector wires shall be kept at least 2 1/2 inches apart and, where the span exceeds eighty feet, insulating saddles may be placed at intervals not exceeding fifty feet.

d. Sizes of collector wire shall not be less than that shown in the following table:

Distance between rigid supports	Size of wire
0-30 feet	No. 6
31-60 feet	No. 4
Over 60 feet	No. 2

e. Conductors along runways and crane bridges may consist of steel tees, angles, tee-rails, trolley wires or other stiff shapes, rigidly carried by insulating supports spaced at intervals of not more than eighty times the thickness of the conductor, but in no case greater than 15 feet and spaced apart sufficiently to give a clear electrical separation of conductors or adjacent collectors of not less than one inch. All sections of the conductors shall be mechanically joined to provide a continuous electrical connection.

f. Except in locations to which only qualified persons are admitted, collector conductors shall be so isolated by elevation or be provided with suitable guards so arranged that persons cannot inadvertently touch the current carrying parts while in contact with the ground or with conducting material connected to the ground.

Section B30-161.0 - Collectors.

Collectors shall be so designed as to reduce to a minimum the sparking between them and the conductor. Cranes or hoists installed in paper warehouses and in hazardous locations shall be safeguarded in accordance with Article 23 of this title.

Section B30-162.0 - Switches and Cutouts.

a. The main collector wires shall be protected by a cutout and the circuit shall be controlled by a switch. The switch shall be located within sight of the collector wires and shall be readily operable from the floor or ground.

b. Where cranes are operated from cabs, a circuit breaker or switch, capable of interrupting the circuit under heavy loads and readily accessible to the operator shall be provided. Means shall be provided accessible for locking the switch or circuit breaker in the open position and shall be provided in the leads from the main collector wires, unless the current collectors can be safely removed, under heavy loads, from the trolley or third rail.

c. Where more than one motor is employed on a crane, each motor shall have its individual automatic over-current protection in accordance with the provisions of Articles 8 and 10 of this title; provided, however, that where two motors operate a single hoist, carriage, truck or bridge and are controlled as a unit by one controller, the pair of motors with their leads may be protected by a single common automatic current (over) protective device. This cutout shall be located in the cab, if there is one.

d. On both alternating current and direct current crane protective panels, the continuous capacity of the main line switch and main line contactors shall not be less than fifty percent of the combined short time ratings of the motors nor less than seventy-five percent of the short time rating of the largest individual motor.

e. Each hoist motor shall be equipped with an enclosed type limit switch, so placed and arranged as to disconnect the motor and apply the brake in time to stop the motor before the hook passes the highest point of safe travel.

f. Cranes and hoists operated by polyphase alternating current motors shall be protected to prevent starting the motor if:
1. The phase rotation is in the wrong direction, or
2. There is a failure in any phase.

This protection may be placed ahead of the runway feeders.

Section B30-163.0 - Controllers.

a. If the crane operates over inflammable material, the resistors shall be placed in a well-ventilated cabinet, composed of non-combustible material, so constructed that it will not emit flame or molten metal.

b. If the resistors are located in a cab, this requirement may be met by constructing the latter of non-combustible material, enclosing the sides of the cab from the floor to a point at least six inches above the tops of the resistors.

c. Manually operated controllers which are operated from the floor with *shipper ropes* shall be provided with means for automatically returning the controller to the *off* position when released by the operator. Controllers in cabs shall be so located that the operator can readily face the direction of travel.

Section B30-164.0 - Grounding.

Motor frames, tracks, and the entire frame of the crane shall be grounded as prescribed in Article 9 of this title. (Class III location)

Section B30-174.0 - Hazardous Locations.

a. Lamps shall not be installed in locations where they are exposed to mechanical injury when bales are being tiered or handled. Lighting fixtures shall be wired with wire not smaller than No. 14, and the fixture wiring shall be enclosed in rigid conduit. Lamps may be in receptacles attached directly to the outlet box covers. Lamps and their lamp holders shall be so enclosed that in the event of a burnout of the lamp or lamp holder, no spark or hot metal can escape from the enclosure.

b. Electric cranes operating in a warehouse or other building shall not be operated on a system with a grounded conductor. Feeders for electric cranes shall be provided with a recording ground detector and protected by a relay which will automatically open the feeders circuit breaker in the event of the insulation of the system failing below one thousand ohms. Bare conductors for such cranes shall be protected by suitable barriers so arranged as to prevent any escape of sparks or hot particles and the moving current collectors shall be so designed as to minimize sparking at sliding contacts. Where the distance of travel permits, current to the crane shall be supplied through type S or type BA flexible portable conductors, equipped with a type of reel or takeup device approved for the purpose.

    c. Storage battery charging equipment shall be located in separate rooms built of or lined with substantial non-combustible materials, so constructed as to exclude dust and shall be well-ventilated. No storage battery shall be charged except in such room.

    d. The wheels of electric trucks entering Class III locations shall be provided with rubber tires or made of non-conducting material.

1. Wiring other than bare collector wires shall be rubber covered, slow-burning (type S.B.), or

    A. varnish cambric (type V)
    B. asbestos covered (type A)
    C. asbestos varnished cambric (type AVA)
    D. asbestos varnished cambric (type AVB)

2. Rubber covered wire (except on pilot circuits of controllers, where No. 14 may be used) shall NOT be smaller than No.

    A. 12   B. 10   C. 8   D. 6

3. Wires exposed to external heat in excess of 122° F. (50° C.) shall be

    A. asbestos covered (type V)
    B. fire resistant (type R.P.)
    C. slow-burning (type S.B.)
    D. double braid rubber

4. Collector wires

    A. may be used as feeders for any equipment other than crane, provided they are properly fused
    B. should not be used as feeders for any equipment other than the crane or cranes which they are primarily designed to serve
    C. shall not be smaller than No. 14 A.W.G.
    D. shall have a capacity of not less than half the capacity of the fuse

5. The use of common return wires for two or more motors is

    A. permitted
    B. not permitted
    C. permitted if installed in rigid conduit
    D. permitted if wires so used are bunched

6. The size of collector wire having a distance between rigid supports not greater than 30' should NOT be less than _____ A.W.G.

    A. No. 3   B. No. 4   C. No. 5   D. No. 6

7. Crane and hoists operated by poly-phase alternating current shall be protected in order to prevent starting the motor if the phase rotation is

    A. in the right direction   B. clockwise
    C. in the wrong direction   D. counterclockwise

5 (#1)

8. The MAIN collector wires should be prevented and protected by a cutout and the circuit controlled by a(n) 8.____

   A. reverse current relay
   B. thermo cutout
   C. undervoltage relay
   D. switch

9. Bridge collector wires shall be kept AT LEAST _____ apart. 9.____

   A. 2" B. $2\frac{1}{4}$" C. $2\frac{1}{2}$" D. 2 3/4"

10. Cranes and hoists operated by poly-phase alternating current motors shall be protected to prevent starting the motor 10.____

    A. if there is a failure in any phase
    B. when the brake circuit is energized
    C. when the motor secondary resistance is all in
    D. when the power factor is less than unity

KEY (CORRECT ANSWERS)

1. B
2. A
3. C
4. D
5. B

6. D
7. B
8. D
9. C
10. A

EXAMINATION SECTION
TEST 1

DIRECTIONS: In continuous discourse, answer the following questions concisely and briefly.

1. A crawler mounted crane is to be used in hoisting concrete buckets to the top of a building during the course of erection of the building. The crane has a 100 ft. boom with a 20 ft. jib. Assume that you are an inspector and that you are to inspect this crane to determine whether it is safe to use for this job. Describe how you would make this inspection and all the features of the crane that you would check in this inspection. If, in your answer, you make reference to a specific crane, give the name and model number of the crane you refer to.

2. A. Describe completely how an eye should be made in wire rope using Crosby clips. Be sure to include how the number and spacing of clips is determined.
   B. State the principal use of a wedge socket and describe or illustrate by a simple sketch how this socket should be made up.

3. Describe how you would inspect a set of chain falls to determine whether they were safe to use. What defects would be cause for condemning the falls?

4. Describe or illustrate by a simple sketch, each of the following types of slings and state or show how each would be used in a rigging job:

   A. Endless sling
   C. Four-leg bridle sling
   B. Chocker sling
   D. Equalizing Sling

5. Waterproofers are using a swinging scaffold to point the brick wall of a 5-story building. You have been assigned to inspect this operation to determine whether the rigging has been done properly and whether the rigging gear is safe to use. Describe how you would make this inspection and all the items you would check.

6. A. 1. Give the basic differences in the method of making up a short splice as compared to a long splice.
      2. When is each type of splice used?

   B. State the MOST frequent use of each of the following knots:
      1. Sheet bend
      2. Rolling hitch
      3. Blackwall hitch
      4. Running bowline
      5. Clove hitch

7. A heavy piece of printing machinery is being lifted by crane to the third floor of a building. On attempting to get the machine through the third floor window, the load slipped, falling to the ground and injuring a man. You are asked, as an inspector, to investigate this accident. Write a report to the Chief Inspector covering the items you have investigated and your findings. You may make any assumptions necessary to properly answer this question. DO NOT SIGN YOUR NAME. Sign the report "John Doe." If you sign in any other manner your paper will not be rated.

8. Describe, or illustrate by a simple sketch, each of the following types of hoisting rigs, and give the principal use of each.

    A. Gin role
    B. Shear legs
    C. Guyed derrick
    D. Cat head

9. A 4-ton load is being lifted with manila rope using one double block and one triple block.

    A. Compute the mechanical advantage.
    B. What is the actual pull required?
    C. What is the smallest safe size (diameter) manila rope that can be used for this job?
    D. What size blocks should be used for this job?

    Note: Show how you arrived at your answers. Answers without method will receive no credit.

10. A piece of heavy machinery is being transferred across an air shaft from one building to a lower floor in another building. There is no access from the front of the building.

    A. State how this job should be done and what equipment should be used.
    B. As an inspector interested in the safe completion of this job, what inspections would you make and what items would you check?

TEST 2

DIRECTIONS: In continuous discourse, answer the following questions concisely and briefly.

1. A. Give 4 knots generally used in the tying of manila rope.
   B. What knot should be used to join ropes of unequal size?
   C. What knot should be used to hoist a spar?
   D. What knot should be used to attach a single rope to a hook of a block for hoisting?
   E. Describe how any one of the above knots should be tied.

2. A. As an inspector on a job on which manila rope is being used, give 5 details concerning the rope which you would check.
   B. What inspection would you make of a chain?

3. A. What is a snatch block?
   B. What is a "deadman"?
   C. What is a "holdfast"?
   D. How would you determine the lifting capacity of a given tackle?
   E. What inspection should be made of hooks, sheaves, and blocks?

4. A. How would you determine the capacity of cables or chains?
   B. What action would you take as an inspector, if you found cables being used in close proximity to the working area?
   C. What inspection should be made of cable?
   D. How should cables be fastened to an object?

5. Describe or sketch the following types of derricks;

   A. Gin Pole
   B. Guy derrick
   C. Stiff leg derrick
   D. A-frame derrick

6. A. What kind of lumber and timber may be used for scaffolding?
   B. What defects would you look for in the above timber?
   C. What inspections and tests would you make on a swinging scaffold to be used by 2 men?

7. A derrick is to be used on the roof of a building. Describe in detail the items you would check in your inspection.

8. A. What type of signalling should be used in all engine work?
   B. How would you determine the maximum load a hoisting engine can lift?
   C. What capacity brakes would you expect to find on a hoist engine?
   D. What regulations should be enforced concerning workmen riding on material hoists?

9. What protection must be provided for the operator of all engines with respect to:

   A. Falling objects
   B. Internal combustion engine exhuasts
   C. Steam and smoke
   D. Filling of fuel tanks

10. Write a report to your superior outlining a set of specifications that you believe should be enforced in the inspection of hoistways. Sign your report "John Doe."

TEST 3

DIRECTIONS: In continuous discourse, answer the following questions concisely and briefly.

1. A. Explain, in detail, how you would determine whether or not a manila line was in good condition.
    B. How should manila rope be stored?

2. A. List the common causes of cable failure.
    B. What are the three defects in cables any one of which makes it mandatory to discard a cable?

3. A. Give two reasons for lubricating cable.
    B. For best results, how should a cable which is being used in a tackle, be lubricated?

4. A. Explain how a cable should be fastened to a deadman. Give enough detail to enable a man familiar with rope but unfamiliar with cable to perform the job.
    B. Explain how a socket is attached to a cable. How can you determine whether or not the molten zinc is at the proper temperature?

5. A. Why is wrought iron usually preferred to steel as a material for hoisting chains?
    B. Who is permitted to repair chains?
    C. Explain, in detail, how cable should be removed from a reel if
       1. equipment is available
       2. no equipment is available

6. A. What is meant by 'mousing a hook'?
    B. What two purposes does an adequate mousing serve?
    C. A lifting tackle consisting of two double blocks is arranged to give a mechanical advantage of four (neglecting friction). One block has a shackle connection, the other a hook.
    D. Which block should be used for the upper (fixed) block? Why? Give two reasons.

7. A. A penthouse is being constructed on top of an existing six-story building. Steel must be lifted by a crane located on the street. With what rules and regulations must the rigger comply before starting operations? What safety precautions would you, as an Inspector of Hoists and Rigging, insist on in such an operation?
    B. What points would you check to make sure that a hoisting engine on a job complied with the rules of the Board of Standards and Appeals?

8. Two cranes, one with a capacity of 15 tons, the other with a capacity of 25 tons, are to be used to lift a load of 30 tons. An equalizing bar weighing 5 tons and having a spread of 25'-0" is to be used. Where, along the equalizing bar, should the load-lifting eye be placed if the cranes are to be loaded in proportion to their capacities? Show all computations?

9-10. The guy derrick shown below has a 35'-0" mast and a 25'-0" boom. The mast is supported by six guys equally spaced around the mast. Each guy makes an angle of 45° with the horizontal. The boom is midway between two guys.

77

2 (#3)

A. Find the total stress in the boom.
B. Find the total stress in the mast.
C. Find the total stress in each of the leaded guys.
D. What size timber is required for the mast

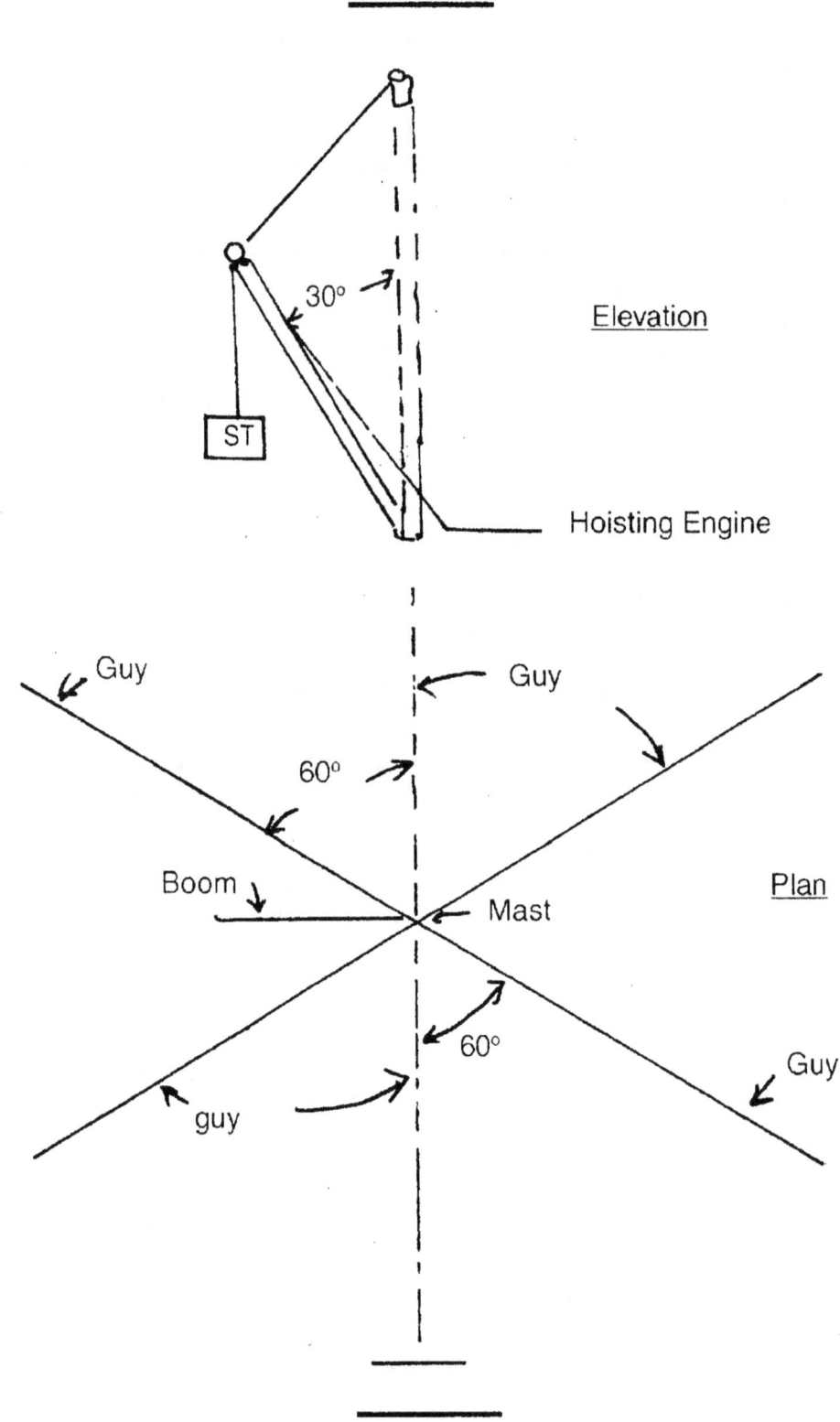

Elevation

Plan

EXAMINATION SECTION
TEST 1

DIRECTIONS: Directly and concisely, using brief answer form, answer the following questions.

1. What are the outside plates of a wire rope block called?
2. What is put on the end of wood piling to keep the hammer?
3. What is a single sheave block called that is open at the hook?
4. What knot is BEST to use when the rope must be shortened but cannot reach the ends?
5. What tool is used in making connections in a raising gang?
6. What do you call the timber put in a guy to keep it from twisting?
7. What is used to lengthen a boom for lifting light loads?
8. What is meant by the expression "three and three"?
9. What is the line on a derrick called that raises the boom?
10. To what do you fasten the shackles on a guy derrick?

2 (#1)

KEY (CORRECT ANSWERS)

1. Check (carrying) plates

2. Bonnet (cap) (ring) (band)

3. Snatch (gate) (foot) block

4. Sheepshank

5. Fork (spud) wrench
   Drift (bull) pin
   Hammer (beater)

6. Monkey tail (monkey)

7. Outrigger
   Jib
   Gooseneck

8. Three sheave blocks at top and bottom

9. Topping lift (boom lift)

10. Spider
    Turnbuckles

TEST 2

DIRECTIONS: Directly and concisely, using brief answer form, answer the following questions.

1. Where do you generally start to reeve up a set of triple blocks for a heavy load?

2. What is a boom called which is fastened to the side of a building, reeved from the top of boom to the building, and swung on a pivot?

3. What knot may serve as a bos'n chair and is also useful in taking the hook of a tackle?

4. On a tiered building, what is the term used for raising the derrick up from one floor to the next?

5. What is putting the last piece of steel on the top of a building called?

6. What is meant by the expression "two blocks"?

7. What is another name for a winch?

8. Name two knots that are used to tie the ends of lines together to make a safe hitch.

9. What is the falsework called that is built up under machinery when unloading it?

10. Name the parts of a stiff-leg derrick, besides the blocks.

KEY (CORRECT ANSWERS)

1. From the center

2. Chicago boom

3. Bowline
   Double bowline

4. Jumping the derrick

5. Topping out

6. When fall block meets top block (as high as can go) (no more pull)

7. Crab
   Niggerhead

8. Two bowlines
   Bowline and two half hitches
   Bowline and becket bend
   Square (hard) (flat)
   Reef
   Fisherman's bend

9. Cribbing

10. Two sills
    Two stiff-legs
    One mast
    One boom

TEST 3

DIRECTIONS: Directly and concisely, using brief answer form, answer the following questions.

1. What is the derrick called that is supported by wire ropes?
2. What do you fasten the dead end of a rope to on a block?
3. What do you call putting lines through blocks?
4. What is the temporary timber or steel support called that is used under a bridge when erecting it?
5. What tool is put between two guy lines so that it can pull on both of them at the same time?
6. What is a sheepshank used for?
7. What devices are there on a winch to hold the load in a given position?
8. Name the four parts of a block.
9. What fastenings are used in handling timber?
10. What is the BEST hitch to use for fastening a hoisting tackle to a vertical rod?

2 (#3)

KEY (CORRECT ANSWERS)

1. Guy derrick
2. Becket (ring) (thimble) (swivel) (eye)
3. Reeving
4. Falsework (cribbing)
5. Steamboat ratchet
   Turnbuckle
6. To shorten lines
7. Dogs (pawls)
8. Sheave
   Hook
   Becket
   Shell
9. Timber hitches
10. Rolling hitch (stopper)

MATERIAL HOISTING

23-6.1 General requirements. (a) *Application of subpart.* The general requirements of this subpart shall apply to all material hoisting equipment except cranes, derricks, aerial baskets, excavating machines used for material hoisting and fork lift trucks.

(b) *Maintenance.* Material hoisting equipment shall at all times be maintained in good repair and proper operating condition with sufficient inspections to insure such maintenance. All defects affecting safety shall be immediately corrected either by necessary repairs or replacement of parts, or such defective equipment shall be immediately removed from the job site.

(c) *Operation.* (1) Only trained, designated persons shall operate hoisting equipment and such equipment shall be operated in a safe manner at all times.

(2) Operators of material hoisting equipment shall remain at the controls while any load is suspended.

(d) *Loading.* Material hoisting equipment shall not be loaded in excess of the live load for which it was designed as specified by the manufacturer. Where there is any hazard to persons, all loads shall be properly trimmed to prevent dislodgment of any portions of such loads during transit. Suspended loads shall be securely slung and properly balanced before they are set in motion.

(e) *Signal system required.* (1) *Operators and signalmen.* Material hoists shall be operated only in response to a signal system and all operators and signalmen shall be able to comprehend the signals readily and to execute them properly.

(2) *Signal transmittal.* Such signal system shall consist of manual signals, telephone communications or a visual or audible signal code. Such signaling methods may be used separately or in combination. Where manual or visual signals are used, the signalman shall have a clear and unobstructed view of the hoist operator at all times and the hoist operator shall have a clear and unobstructed view of the signalman at all times. The maximum distance between the signalman and the operator shall be 80 feet. Where persons are loading or unloading at more than one level or where the signalman cannot be readily seen by the hoist operator, an electrically- or mechanically-operated bell system shall be provided and used. Where audible signals are used, such signals shall be capable of being heard at all times above the normal sound level in the area. Intercommunication or telephone systems shall be provided in addition to manually-operated electrical or mechanical bell signal systems where necessary for safe operation of the hoist. Weatherproof electrical connections and fittings shall be used for electrically-operated signal or communication systems on hoist towers that are exposed to the elements.

(3) *Visual and audible signal code.* Where 11 visual or audible signal system is used in the operation of any material hoist, the following signal code shall be employed:

Signal	Action
1 bell or light	Stop
2 bells or lights	Raise
3 bells or lights	Lower
4 bells or lights	Lower slowly

(4) *Posting of signal code.* Where a visual or audible signal code is used, a copy of such code shall be posted in a conspicuous location adjacent to the hoisting controls, clearly visible to the hoist operator from his operating position. Where there is a car attendant, such code shall also be posted in a conspicuous position in the hoist car.

[23-6.1]

(f) *Protection of hoist operator.* (1) Where an overhead hazard exists, the operator of a hoisting machine shall be provided with overhead protection equivalent to tight planking not less than two inches thick which is supported to develop its full strength.

(2) The area or space occupied by the hoisting machine and its operator shall be protected from the elements and shall be heated in cold weather to a temperature of at least 60 degrees Fahrenheit at all times such area or space is occupied.

(g) *Protection of moving parts.* Gears, belts, sprockets, drums, sheaves and points of contact between moving parts of power-driven hoist equipment, when not guarded by location, shall be guarded in compliance with this Part (rule) and with the Industrial Code Part (Rule No.) 19.

(h) *Tag line.* Loads which have a tendency to swing or turn freely during hoisting shall be controlled by tag lines.

(i) *Riding.* Riding on loads, buckets, slings, balls or hooks of material hoisting equipment is prohibited.

(j) *Hoisting machine.* (1) *Hoist brakes.* Hoist brakes, capable of stopping and holding 150 per cent of the rated capacity of the hoist, shall be provided for every material hoist. Each manually-operated material hoist shall be equipped with an effective pawl and ratchet capable of holding the rated load capacity when such a load is suspended. Each electric motor-driven material hoist shall be provided with a mechanical automatic motor brake or an electrical or mechanical device which will stop and hold 150 per cent of the rated capacity of the hoist automatically in ease of power failure.

(2) *Hoisting machine anchorage.* Hoisting machines shall be so constructed, installed and secured in place as to prevent tipping or dislodgment.

(k) *Repairs and lubrication.* No repairing, cleaning or lubricating of machinery shall be done unless such machinery is at rest.

23-6.2 Rigging, rope and chains for material hoists. (a) *Hoisting rope.* (1) *Types required.* Only wire rope of the improved plow steel classification or equivalent having a safety factor of not less than six shall be used with power-driven hoisting machinery, except for winch-heads or capstan hoists where fibre rope may be used.

(2) *Fibre rope.* (i) Fibre rope shall be first grade manila hemp or synthetic fibre. Means to prevent chafing shall be provided where necessary. Proper size blocks to accommodate the rope shall be used. Fibre rope shall be protected where acid or any other harmful or corrosive agent or chemical is used. All fibre rope shall be stored in a dry condition and in a dry place protected from the elements.

(ii) Fibre rope that is unsound in any way or that shows the effects of severe wear, deterioration or abrasion shall not be used and shall be removed from the job site. Frozen rope shall be thawed before being used.

(3) *Wire rope.* (i) Wire rope shall be so handled and stored as to prevent kinks and shall be maintained lubricated to prevent corrosion. Wire rope that is kinked shall not be used on any material hoist. Wire rope shall be discarded and replaced when more than 10 per cent of the total wires of any lay are broken. A rope lay is that distance measured along the rope in which one strand makes a complete revolution around the rope axis. Wire rope shall be discarded and replaced when the wires on the crown of the strands are worn down to less than 60 per cent of their original cross-sectional area, when visual inspection indicates marked signs of corrosion, deterioration or abrasion and when any combination of broken wires and abrasion has reduced the original strength of the rope to 80 per cent or less.

[23-6.2]

(ii) The ends of wire rope shall be securely attached to the hoist drums and at least four turns of rope shall remain on each drum at all times.

Exception: Attachment of the rope to the hoist drum shall not be required on traction type hoists.

(iii) Means shall be provided to prevent accidental contact with or damage to any hoisting rope. Such means shall consist of substantial covering, fencing or guarding by location.

(4) *Wire rope fastenings.* (i) Wire rope fastenings shall consist of zinc-filled sockets, wedge sockets with at least one rope clip above each socket, eye-splices with pear-shaped thimbles to fit the rope, proper size thimbles with rope clips or other approved fastenings.

(ii) Where clips are used as fastenings, the number used shall be in accordance with Table XVI of this subpart.

(iii) The spacing between clips shall be at least six times the diameter of the rope. The U-bolts of clips shall be placed over the short ends of the ropes.

TABLE XVI
ROPE CLIP REQUIREMENTS

Rope Diameter	Minimum Number of Clips
Up to and including 7/16 inch	2
Up to and including 5/6 inch	3
Up to and including 1 inch	4
Up to and including 1-1/4 inches	5
Up to and including 1-5/6 inches	6
Up to and including 1-3/4 inches	7
Up to and including 2-1/2 inches	8
Up to and including 3 inches	9

(b) *Sheaves.* Load-bearing sheaves for wire rope shall be of proper diameter and grooving to accommodate the rope but in no case shall such diameter be less than 20 times the diameter of the rope. Sheaves shall be maintained properly lubricated. Sheaves and blocks that are so excessively worn, damaged, deteriorated or otherwise defective as to cause or threaten to cause failure of the equipment shall not be used. Sheaves intended for use with fibre rope shall not be used with wire rope.

(c) *Fittings.* All hooks, shackles and other fittings subject to tension or shear shall be drop-forged. The use of deformed or damaged hooks, shackles, chains or other fittings is prohibited. All suspended pulley blocks, sheaves, well wheels or similar devices shall be moused or securely fastened or safety hooks shall be used.

[23-6.2]

(2) Chains shall not be knotted nor shall they be shortened or spliced by the use of nails or bolts.

(3) Defective chains shall not be used.

(e) *Heat treating of chains.* The annealing or normalizing of chains shall be performed only by the manufacturer or his authorized agent.

23-6.3 Material platform or bucket hoists. (a) *Design requirement.* Every material platform or bucket hoist erected after June 1, 1972 shall be designed by a professional engineer licensed to practice in the State. The design plans and specifications for any such hoist shall be kept on the job site available for examination by the commissioner.

(b) *Material hoist towers.* (1) The tower of every material hoist shall be supported by a firm foundation of such dimensions and area as to adequately distribute the intended load so as not to exceed the safe load-bearing capacity of the supporting soil. Tower bracing shall be constructed of such material and shall be so installed as to secure tower stability and rigidity and to keep the tower plumb.

(2) Each such tower shall be secured with guys or rigid braces at each corner at intervals not to exceed 26 feet vertically. Tower guys shall be at least one-half inch diameter improved plow steel wire rope and shall be securely fastened to adequate anchorages with wire rope clips in accordance with Table XVI of this subpart.

(3) The erection and dismantling of any material hoist tower shall be performed only under the direct supervision of a designated person experienced in this type of work. Timber hoist towers shall be erected only to a height necessary for the performance of the work and shall be extended in height only when the construction work has progressed sufficiently to provide for the anchorages and bracing heretofore required. Hoist towers constructed of metal shall not be erected to a height exceeding 50 feet above the highest portion of the buildings or other structures which may be used as suitable anchorages for guying such towers.

(4) Hoist towers shall be so constructed that there shall be at least four feet of clearance between the lowest point on the circumference of the cathead sheave and the highest point on the hoisting rope fastening on the car or bucket when such conveyance is at the uppermost terminal or landing.

(c) *Hoistway enclosures.* (1) *Interior.* Interior hoistways for material hoists shall be enclosed at every floor level to a height of at least eight feet on all sides except entrance openings. Such enclosures shall be constructed of wire mesh of not less than No. 18 U.S. gage steel with openings which will reject a one-half inch diameter ball or such enclosures shall be partitions of exterior grade plywood at least three-quarters inch thick, of wood slats not less than three-quarters inch thick installed horizontally and spaced not more than two inches apart or of other material of equivalent strength. Such enclosures shall be adequately supported, braced and secured.

(2) *Enclosed exterior.* When any exterior hoistway for a material hoist is enclosed, such enclosure shall extend from the lowest terminal points to the cathead elevations on all sides except entrance openings. Such enclosure shall be constructed of wire mesh of not less than No. 18 U.S. gage steel with openings which will reject a one-half inch diameter ball.

(3) *Unenclosed exterior.* When any exterior hoistway for a material hoist is unenclosed, the following requirements shall apply:

[23-6.3]

(i) Such hoistway shall be enclosed at the ground or grade level to a height of at least six feet on all sides except entrance openings. Such enclosure shall be constructed of wire mesh of not less than No. 18 U.S. gage steel with openings which will reject a one-half inch diameter ball. Entrance openings of any such hoistway shall be provided with gates or bars in compliance with this Part (rule) except that sliding bars may be used in lieu of hinged bars. Such gates or bars shall be kept closed whenever the car is hoisted.

(ii) In addition to the enclosure of the hoist car as required by this Part (rule), each loading side of any such car shall be provided with a self-closing gate at least 66 inches in height, constructed of the same material as the car enclosure.

(iii) Where any point on a moving car or counterweight of a material hoist passes less than eight feet from a floor, roof, scaffold platform or other work surface or position, such floor, roof, scaffold platform or other work surface shall be provided with a partition at least six feet in height. Such partition shall extend horizontally at least five feet past the horizontal projection of the path of the car or counterweight. Such partition shall be at least equal in construction to hoistway enclosures as specified in this Part (rule).

(d) *Entrances to hoistways.* (1) All entrances to any hoistway used for material hoisting above the lowest loading terminal or grade entrance shall be guarded by substantial gates painted fluorescent orange or yellow. When closed, such gates shall guard the full width of the entrance openings. The top of each such gate shall be at least 36 inches in height above the floor surface when located two feet or more from the hoistway line. Any such gate located less than two feet from the hoistway line shall be not less than 66 inches in height above the floor surface. If such entrance gates are constructed with a grille, wire mesh, lattice or other openwork material, the openings therein shall reject a ball more than two inches in diameter. Any such gate shall have an underclearance of not more than two inches. Such entrance gates shall be either verical sliding, horizontal sliding or swinging gates. Any swinging gate shall swing in the direction of egress from the car to the floor.

(2) At the lowest loading terminal or grade entrance, a wood or metal bar may be used to guard the entrance to a hoistway used for material hoisting. Such bar shall be painted fluorescent orange or yellow. Such bar shall be mechanically or electrically interlocked with the hoist car so that the bar shall be closed and locked before the car can leave the lowest terminal or grade level and cannot be opened until the ear has returned to such level.

(3) Bars or pipes shall not be used to guard hoistway entrances at any level or floor above the lowest terminal or grade level.

(4) Gates at hoistway entrances above the lowest terminal or grade level shall be kept closed when the car is not at such entrances.

(e) *Car construction.* (1) Hoist cars used for material hoisting shall be enclosed from floor to crosshead with solid enclosures on all sides not used for loading or unloading. Every such hoist car shall be provided with overhead protection installed at the crosshead to protect any person from falling objects or materials. Such overhead protection shall consist of planking at least two inches thick, exterior grade plywood at least three-quarters inch thick or other material of equivalent strength.

(2) In lieu of solid enclosures, hoist cars may be enclosed with expanded metal of not less than No. 9 U.S. gage steel with openings which will reject a one and one-half inch diameter ball. Such enclosed cars shall also be provided with toeboards at least four inches in height on all sides except those used for loading and unloading.

(3) Car platforms shall be provided with securely fastened blocks and cleats to prevent the rolling of wheeled vehicles and the shifting of other equipment.

[23-6.3]

(f) *Guide rails.* The guide rails of material hoists shall be constructed of steel or sound, structural grade hardwood securely fastened at intervals so as not to deflect more than one-quarter inch during normal operation of the hoist.

(g) *Operation of hoist.* The operation of any hoist car, bucket or platform is prohibited whenever persons are climbing the hoist tower or working on any part of the tower below the cathead.

> *Exception:* The platform, cage, car or bucket may be used to raise persons for authorized maintenance and repairs that cannot be done otherwise.

(h) *Protection of operator.* The operator of every hoisting machine used with material platform or bucket hoists shall be provided with overhead protection against falling objects or materials. Such overhead protection shall be equivalent to tight planking not less than two inches thick supported to develop its full strength.

(i) *Loading and roping of platform hoists.* The maximum safe capacity of each platform hoist shall be determined by using a factor of safety of eight. Such maximum capacity shall be posted conspicuously on the crosshead or side members of every such hoist and such capacity shall not be exceeded.

(j) *Thoroughfare.* Hoistways for material hoists shall not be located either partially or wholly over sidewalks, passageways or other areas to which persons have access unless a broken-rope safety device is provided for each such hoistway. Such safety devices shall be capable of stopping and holding the platform or bucket with its rated load. Such safety device requirement shall also apply to the counterweights of such hoists, if provided.

(k) *Riding.* Riding by any person on a material hoist is prohibited except for necessary inspection, maintenance and repairs. Signs to that effect shall be posted in conspicuous locations on both side of the crosshead or side members and at every entrance to any such hoist. The legend on every such sign, in letters not less than one and one-half inches in height on contrasting backgrounds, shall read as follows:

"WARNING -- RIDING BY ANY PERSON PROHIBITED"

PERSONNEL HOISTS

23-7.1 General requirements. (a) *Application of subpart.* This subpart applies to personnel hoists where the temporary use of permanent elevators is made or where temporary workmen's hoists are provided to transport persons to and from their working levels in the construction of buildings or other structures.

(b) *Maintenance.* Personnel hoisting equipment shall be maintained in good repair and in proper operating condition at all times. Inspections of such equipment shall be made with such frequency as to insure such maintenance and operation.

(c) *Operation.* Only trained, designated persons shall operate personnel hoists and such hoists shall be operated in a safe manner at all times.

23-7.2 Temporary personnel or workmen's hoists. (a) *Approval required.* Temporary personnel hoists shall not be placed in service until each such installation has been granted a special approval. The requirements of any such approval shall be applied in conjunction with all other requirements of this section.

(b) *Hoist towers.* (1) Every hoist tower used for a temporary personnel hoist shall be supported by a firm foundation of such dimensions as to adequately distribute the transmitted load so as not to exceed the safe load-bearing capacity of the ground upon which such tower is erected. Each such hoist tower shall be securely braced to the building or other structure so that such tower is held in a plumb vertical position, is stable, rigid and able to withstand wind pressure.

(2) Each such hoist tower shall be secured with guys or rigid braces at each corner at intervals not to exceed 26 feet vertically. Tower guys shall be at least one-half inch diameter improved plow steel wire rope and shall be securely fastened to adequate anchorages with wire rope clips as specified in Table XVI, Support 23-6, of this Part (rule). All building tie-ins shall be identified by metal tags bearing the legend: "WORKMEN'S HOIST-DO NOT REMOVE."

(3) Hoist towers shall be erected and dismantled only under the direct supervision of qualified, designated persons.

(4) Hoist towers shall be erected only to heights necessary for the performance of the work and shall be extended in height only when construction has progressed sufficiently in height in order to provide for the adequate anchorages and bracing required by this subpart unless other safe and adequate guying can be provided.

(c) *Hoistway enclosures.* (1) *Interior.* Interior hoistways for temporary personnel hoists shall be fully enclosed at every floor except for entrance openings. Such enclosures shall be constructed of wire mesh of not less than No. 18 U.S. gage steel with openings which will reject a one-half inch diameter ball or such enclosures shall be partitions of exterior grade plywood at least three-eighths inch thick, of wood slats not less than three-quarters inch thick installed horizontally and spaced not more than two inches apart or of other material of equivalent strength. Such enclosures shall be adequately supported, braced and secured.

(2) *Enclosed exterior.* When exterior hoistways for personnel hoists are enclosed, such enclosures shall extend from the lowest terminal points to the cathead elevations on all sides except entrance openings. Such enclosures shall be constructed of wire mesh of not less than No. 18 U.S. gage steel with openings which will reject a one-half inch diameter ball.

[23-7.2]

(3) *Unenclosed exterior.* When exterior hoistways for personnel hoists are unenclosed, the following requirements shall apply:

(i) Every such hoistway shall be enclosed at the ground or grade level to a height of at least ten feet on all sides except entrance openings. Such enclosures shall be constructed of wire mesh of not less than No. 18 U.S. gage steel with openings which will reject a one-half inch diameter ball. The entrance openings of such hoistways shall be guarded in compliance with this section.

(ii) Where any point on a moving car or counterweight passes less than eight feet from a floor, scaffold platform or other work surface or position, such floor, scaffold platform or other work surface so exposed shall be provided with a partition at least six feet in height. Such partition shall extend horizontally at least five feet past the horizontal projection of the path of the car or counterweight. Such partition shall be at least equal in construction to hoistway enclosures as specified in this section.

(4) *Running clearances.* Every hoistway enclosure shall be so installed and reinforced in all areas subject to external pressure that the running clearances between car and enclosure cannot be reduced to less than one inch upon the application of any horizontal pressure of 100 pounds against any point on such enclosure.

(d) *Hoistway doors.* (1) Every entrance opening in any hoistway enclosure for a personnel hoist shall be provided with a solid door at least 78 inches in height which shall extend across the full width of the opening. Such door shall be provided with a vision panel securely covered with wire mesh. Such door shall be provided with a lock or latch which is openable from the hoistway side only and inaccessible from the landing side. Every such door shall have an underclearance of not more than one-half inch.

> *Exception:* Such entrance door at the lowest landing of any hoistway shall be provided with a means, accessible only to designated persons, for unlocking the door from the landing side.

(2) In normal service every hoistway door shall be locked or latched shut except when in use for passage to or from the car. No person except the car attendant shall open any such door.

(3) Hoistway entrance doors shall be hung to provide durability and shall be securely reinforced.

(e) *Car enclosures.* The car of every personnel hoist shall be permanently enclosed on all sides and the top except the side used for entrance or exit. Such enclosure shall be equivalent in strength to two-inch planking laid tight. The top of every such enclosure shall be provided with an emergency exit opening fitted with a hinged hatch cover. Such exit opening shall be not less than 16 inches in its smallest dimension and not less than 400 square inches in area.

(f) *Car doors or gates.* (1) Each landing side of any car used in a personnel hoist shall be provided with a door or gate at least six feet in height constructed of material at least as equivalent in strength as the car enclosure.

(2) Every opening in such door or gate shall be of such size and shape as to reject a three-inch diameter ball at any point.

(3) Every such car shall be equipped with an approved electrical contact so arranged that the car cannot be operated unless each door or gate is shut.

(g) *Wiring.* Wiring and other electrical equipment shall be of proper quality and properly installed. Electrical installations shall be in accordance with the 1971 National Electrical Code. Hoistway wiring may consist of heavy-duty rubber-covered traveling cable. All wiring and other electrical equipment exposed to the elements shall be weatherproof.

[23-7.2]

(h) *Lighting.* Inside the hoistway car and at each landing means for artificial lighting shall be provided. The insides of hoistway cars, landings and spaces occupied by hoisting machines shall be illuminated in compliance with this Part (rule) at all times.

(i) Materials carried on personnel hoists. Personnel hoists may be used for carrying material providing the rated load capacity of the hoists are not exceeded. When materials are being carried on such a hoist, only the person necessary for handling such materials shall be permitted to ride in the car, in addition to the operator. When concentrated loads are carried in such a hoist car, such loads shall not exceed 25 per cent of the rated load.

(j) *Car attendant or operator.* (1) Any car of a temporary personnel hoist shall not be operated in service unless such car is in charge of a designated person stationed in the car as its attendant or operator.

(2) No person other than such car attendant shall cause or permit the car to move or shall open any car door or gate or hoistway door. The car attendant shall not cause the car to move until he is sure that the car door or gate and the hoistway doors are closed.

(3) The car attendant shall not cause the car to move unless he is satisfied that the load being carried is prepared for movement.

(4) Persons designated as car attendants for temporary personnel hoists shall be over 18 years of age, trained, qualified and competent to operate the cars of such hoists.

(k) *Hoisting machine enclosures.* Where a hoisting machine is located inside a building or other structure, such machine shall be effectively guarded in compliance with this Part (rule). Where a hoisting machine is located outside a building or other structure, such machine shall be enclosed or barricaded in compliance with this Part (rule) and, in addition, shall be provided with substantial overhead protection. Such overhead protection shall consist of planking at least two inches thick full size, exterior grade plywood at least three-quarters inch thick or material of equivalent strength.

(l) *Communications.* A means of voice communication shall be provided for every temporary personnel hoist where such hoist is operated jointly by a car attendant and a hoisting machine operator stationed adjacent to the hoisting machine.

(m) *Inspection and testing.* Prior to use, initially and after any extension, every temporary personnel hoist shall be tested. Such testing shall be performed only by a designated person and shall consist of the following:

(1) A running test with rated load and at rated speed with stops at each landing.

(2) A test of the normal and final terminal stopping devices with no load carried in the upward direction and with full load carried in the downward direction.

(3) A test of the car safety device at rated load and at rated speed.

(4) A test of the car speed governor.

(5) A complete written report of every such test shall be made and signed by the designated person making such tests. Such reports shall include the dates of the tests, the test loads and speeds involved and the results of such tests. Such reports shall be kept in a log book on the job site available for examination by the commissioner.

23-7.3 Temporary use of permanent elevators. (a) *Temporary use permitted.* Passenger or freight elevators being installed in buildings or other structures for permanent use may be used before completion of the building or other structure during construction to carry persons or material, or both, provided such elevators conform to the following requirements:

(b) *Hoistway enclosures.* The hoistway of any such elevator shall be enclosed with its permanent enclosure and permanent doors or such hoistway shall be enclosed with either solid or openwork material, except for access openings, as follows:

[23-7.3]

(1) Openwork enclosures shall be either wire mesh of at least No. 18 U.S. gage steel or expanded metal of at least No. 18 U.S. gage. The openings of such openwork material shall reject a one-half inch diameter ball. Such enclosures shall be provided with unperforated kick plates installed at every floor level above the lowest floor. Where a counterweight is provided such openwork enclosure shall be covered on the counterweight side with wire mesh of not less than No. 18 U.S. gage steel with openings that will reject a one-half inch diameter ball. Such mesh covering shall extend the full width of the counterweight plus one foot on each side.

(2) Solid enclosures shall consist of partitions of exterior grade plywood at least three-eighths inch thick or of other material of equivalent strength.

(3) Every such enclosure shall be so supported and braced that when subjected to a horizontal pressure of 100 pounds applied at any point the resulting deflection shall not exceed one inch and shall not reduce the running clearance to less than one inch.

(c) *Hoistway doors.* Where permanent hoistway doors are not in place, temporary hoistway doors shall be provided as follows:

(1) Every floor landing opening in a hoistway enclosure shall be provided with a solid door extending across the full width of the opening and not less than 78 inches in height. The clearance between the bottom of any such door and the floor shall be not less than one inch nor more than two inches. Each such door shall be provided with a vision panel of not more than 80 square inches in area. Every such vision panel shall be covered with wire mesh of No. 18 U.S. gage steel with openings which will reject a one-half inch diameter ball. Each such hoistway door shall be provided with a lock or latch which is openable from the hoistway side only and inaccessible from the landing side.

(2) If the hoistway door at the lowest terminal landing is locked automatically when closed with the car at the landing, such door shall be provided with a means to unlock it from the landing side to permit access to the car. Such means shall be accessible only to designated persons.

(3) Where such hoistway doors are of the vertical sliding type, they shall be of a type that requires counterweights. Provisions shall be made for the containment of the counterweights if their means of suspension should fail.

(d) *Elevator car.* Except where permanent elevator cars are used, temporary elevator cars used in permanent hoistways shall be constructed to conform to the following requirements:

(1) *Frame.* The frame of every such car shall consist of a safety plank and vertical stiles gusseted to a crosshead constructed of steel channels. Such frame shall be designed and constructed to carry safely all the loads intended to be imposed thereon. Steel diagonal bracing shall be provided to support the four corners of the car-platform.

(2) *Platform.* The platform of every such car shall consist of a channel steel or aluminum frame and steel or aluminum stringers assembled as a unit and secured to the safety plank. Platform flooring shall be constructed of steel or aluminum plate or of wood. If wood is used, it shall be of structural grade lumber not less than two inches thick and shall be protected on the underside by steel sheeting of at least No. 26 U.S. steel. Such flooring shall be securely fastened to the car platform.

(3) *Car enclosures.* Such temporary elevator cars shall be enclosed on the top and on all sides except those sides used as entrance and exit openings. Such enclosures shall consist of planking at least two inches thick, laid tight, or of other material of equivalent strength. The top of every such elevator car shall have an emergency exit opening in the enclosure of not less than 400 square inches in area with the least dimension at least 16 inches. Such emergency exit openings shall be provided with hinged hatch covers.

[23-7.3]

(4) *Car doors or gates.* (i) Each such car shall be provided with car door or gate on the landing side. Such door or gate shall be at least six feet in height and shall be of construction equivalent in strength to that of the car enclosure.

(ii) Every opening in such car door or gate shall be of such size and shape as to reject a three-inch diameter ball.

(iii) Every such car door or gate shall be equipped with an approved electric contact so arranged that the ear cannot be operated unless the door or gate is within two inches of full closure. Such electric contact shall not be readily accessible from within the car.

(iv) Such car doors or gates shall be of the horizontally or counterweighted vertically sliding type. Where a horizontal gate is used, such gate may be arranged to swing inward when fully collapsed.

(5) *Car controls.* The car controls of such elevators shall be so arranged that such cars can be operated or controlled only from within the ears.

(e) *Elevator operators.* Such elevator cars shall be operated only by competent, trained, designated persons.

(f) *Testing.* Prior to the initial use of any temporary elevator installed in a permanent hoistway, such elevator shall be tested by a designated person. Such testing shall be in accordance with the following requirements:

(1) The car of such elevator shall be loaded to its rated capacity and operated at its rated speed to the upper and lower limits of its travel at least twice in order to test the operation of the upper and lower automatic limit devices as well as the operation of the hoisting machine brake at various levels of the hoistway.

(2) With the rated load in place, the car safeties shall be actuated by tripping the governor by hand while the car is traveling downward at rated speed.

(3) Such test shall be repeated with no load at least once every month while the elevator is in use by operating at a slow speed and tripping the governor by hand.

(4) A written report of each test shall be made and signed by the designated person making such tests. Such reports shall include the dates, test loads and speeds involved as well as the test results. Such written reports shall be kept in a log book on the job site available for examination by the commissioner.

MOBILE CRANES, TOWER CRANES AND DERRICKS

23-8.1 General provisions. (a) *Stability and strength.* Mobile cranes, tower cranes and derricks used in construction, demolition and excavation operations shall be so constructed, placed and operated as to be stable. No component or part of any such crane or derrick shall be stressed beyond its rated capacity as determined by the manufacturer or builder.

(b) *Inspection.* (1) Every mobile crane, tower crane and derrick shall be thoroughly inspected by a competent, designated employee or authorized agent of the owner or lessee of such mobile crane, tower crane or derrick at intervals not exceeding one month. Such inspections shall include but not be limited to all blocks, shackles, sheaves, wire rope, connectors, the various devices on the mast or boom, hooks, controls and braking mechanisms.

(2) A written, dated and signed record of each such inspection shall be completed by the competent, designated employee or authorized agent who made the inspection on an inspection form provided by the commissioner. The most recent record of inspection of a mobile crane, tower crane or derrick shall be posted inside the cab of such crane or derrick under a transparent protective covering or shall be filed in an office on the job site available for examination by the commissioner. Attached to such record of inspection shall be a written designation naming the competent employee or authorized agent. Such attached designation shall be signed by the owner or lessee of such mobile crane, tower crane or derrick.

(3) Every mobile crane, tower crane and derrick shall be inspected before being erected or operated for the first time on any job.

(4) Adjustments and repairs to mobile cranes, tower cranes and derricks shall be made only by competent, designated persons.

(5) A preventive maintenance program shall be established for each mobile crane, tower crane and derrick based on the manufacturer's recommendations. Dated and detailed records of such programs shall be available on the job site for examination by the commissioner.

(c) *Footings.* A firm footing shall be provided for every mobile crane, tower crane and derrick.

(d) *Hoisting mechanism brakes and locking devices.* (1) Every power-operated mobile crane, tower crane and derrick shall be provided with hoisting mechanism brakes capable of sustaining at rest one and one-half times the maximum rated load on a single part line. Hand- or foot-operated brakes shall be provided with a substantial locking device to lock any such brake in engagement. Pedals of foot-operated brakes shall be constructed so that the operators' feet cannot easily slip off. Non-slip pedal surfaces are acceptable for this purpose.

(2) Power-controlled lowering devices, when provided, shall be capable of handling rated loads and speeds in order to provide precision lowering and reduce demands on the brake loads.

Exception: This paragraph does not apply to any mobile crane provided with a clamshell or dragline used in excavation operations.

(3) Electrically-driven mobile cranes, tower cranes and derricks shall be provided with devices which will automatically hold the loads in cases of power failure.

(e) *Load handling.* (1) Mobile cranes, tower cranes and derricks shall not be loaded beyond their rated capacities.

[23-8.1]

(2) Hoisting ropes for concrete buckets used with mobile cranes, tower cranes or derricks shall be provided with safety hooks or closed shackles.

(3) Where slings are used to hoist material of long length, spreader bars shall be used to space and keep the sling legs in proper balance.

(4) Reinforcing rods, conduit and lumber, when of uneven lengths as well as column clamps and similar items which cannot be easily secured to form safe drafts or loads shall be hoisted in boxes. Each such box shall be substantially constructed and supported from its four corners by individual lengths of wire rope having spliced or clipped loops for attachment to the load line. The construction and suspension of each such box shall be capable of holding at least four times the load for which it is intended.

(5) In steel erection, when a load is suspended from a mobile crane, tower crane or derrick at two or more points with slings, the eyes of the lifting legs of the slings shall be shackled together and this shackle or the eyes of the shackled slings shall be placed on the hook. Alternatively, the eyes of the lifting legs may be shackled directly to the hoisting block, ball or balance beam. The eyes may be placed on the lifting hook without shackles if the hook is of the safety type.

(6) No more than one load shall be suspended from the same load line of a mobile crane, tower crane or derrick at one time.

(f) *Hoisting the load.* (1) Before starting to hoist with a mobile crane, tower crane or derrick the following inspection for unsafe conditions shall be made:

(i) The hoisting rope shall be free from kinks.

(ii) Multiple part lines shall not be twisted around each other.

(iii) The hook shall be brought over the load in such manner and location as to prevent the load from swinging when hoisting is started.

(iv) The load is well secured and properly balanced in the sling or lifting device before it is lifted more than a few inches.

(v) If there is a slack rope condition, it shall be determined that the hoisting rope is properly seated on the drum and in the sheaves.

(2) During the hoisting operation the following conditions shall be met:

(i) There shall be no sudden acceleration or deceleration of the moving load unless required by emergency conditions.

(ii) The load shall not contact any obstruction.

(3) The side loading of booms on mobile cranes, tower cranes and derricks shall be limited to freely suspended loads.

(4) Mobile cranes, tower cranes and derricks shall not be used for dragging loads sideways.

(5) Mobile cranes, tower cranes and derricks shall not hoist, lower, swing or travel while any person is located on the load or hook.

(6) Mobile cranes, tower cranes and derricks shall not hoist or carry any load over and above any person except as otherwise provided in this Part (rule).

(7) The operator of any mobile crane, tower crane or derrick shall not leave his position at the controls while any load is suspended nor shall any person be permitted to work or pass under a stationary suspended load.

[23-8.1]

(g) *Limitations on modifications of mobile cranes, tower cranes or derricks.* No load-bearing component or part of any mobile crane, tower crane or power-driven derrick shall be replaced by another component or part nor shall any mobile crane, tower crane or derrick be modified by the addition thereto or the removal therefrom of any load-bearing component or part unless such replacement or modification shall be as certified by either the manufacturer or builder of such crane or derrick or by a professional engineer licensed to practice in the State of New York.

(h) *Cast iron.* Cast iron shall not be used for members or parts of any mobile crane, tower crane or derrick subject to tension or torsion except for brake and clutch drums.

(i) *Guarding moving parts.* Exposed moving components or parts of mobile cranes, tower cranes and derricks such as gears, set screws, projection keys, chains, chain sprockets and reciprocating parts which might constitute a hazard under normal operating conditions shall be guarded and such guards shall be securely fastened in place. Each such guard shall be capable of supporting without permanent distortion the weight of a 200 pound man, unless such guard is located where it is impossible for a person to step or ply his weight on it.

(j) *Protection from the elements.* Friction brakes and clutches of mobile cranes, tower cranes and derricks shall be provided with adequate protection from the elements.

(k) *Wire ropes and reeving accessories. (1) Rope safety factors.* Wire rope provided for use on any mobile crane, tower crane or derrick shall be in compliance with the safety factor requirements listed as follows:

(i) For supporting rated loads (including boom suspensions):

(a) The safety factor for live or running ropes that wind on drums or pass over sheaves shall be not less than 3.5.

(b) The safety factor for boom pendants or standing ropes shall be not less than 3.0.

(ii) For supporting the boom and working attachments at recommended travel or transit positions and boom lengths:

(a) The safety factor for live or running ropes shall be not less than 3.5.

(b) The safety factor for boom pendants and standing ropes shall be not less than 3.0.

(iii) For supporting the boom under recommended boom erection conditions:

(a) The safety factor for live or running ropes shall be not less than 3.0.

(b) The safety factor for boom pendants or standing ropes shall be not less than 2.5.

(iv) The safety factors specified in subparagraphs (i), (ii) and (iii) above shall be determined on the basis of rope loads resulting from crane or derrick manufacturers' ratings, with approved reeving, published nominal breaking strengths of new ropes and with load and boom stationary.

(2) *Hoisting rope.* When the hook of the hoist of any mobile crane, tower crane or derrick is resting on the ground or equivalent elevation at least two full wraps of the hoisting rope shall remain on the drum of such crane or derrick.

(3) *Replacement rope.* Replacement ropes for any mobile crane, tower crane or derrick shall be at least the equivalent in strength and grade as the original ropes furnished by the manufacturer or builder of such crane or derrick.

(4) *Eye splices.* Eye splices shall be made in an acceptable manner and rope thimbles shall be used in the eye.

[23-8.1]

(5) *U-bolt clips.* U-bolt clips shall have the U-bolt section on the dead or short end, and the saddle on the live or long end of the rope. Spacing and number of clips shall be in accordance with the manufacturer's recommendation. Clips shall be of drop-forged steel. When a newly installed rope has been in operation for at least one hour, all nuts on the clip bolts shall be re-tightened and they shall be re-checked for tightness at monthly intervals thereafter.

(6) *Special fittings.* Swaged, compressed or wedge-socket fittings shall be applied as recommended by the manufacturer of the rope or fittings or by the manufacturer or builder of the mobile crane, tower crane or derrick.

(7) *Rope inspection.* (i) *Daily.* All running ropes in continuous service on a mobile crane, tower crane or derrick shall be visually inspected at least once every working day.

(ii) *Monthly.* All ropes in use on a mobile crane, tower crane or derrick shall be thoroughly inspected by a competent, designated person at least once a month. A full written, dated and signed report of each such inspection, which shall include the condition of all ropes, shall be kept on file on the job site available for examination by the commissioner. Any rope damage or deterioration which might result in appreciable loss of original rope strength shall be carefully noted and a determination shall be made by the designated person as to whether continued use of such damaged or deteriorated rope constitutes a hazard.

(1) *Lubrication.* (1) *Sheave bearings.* All sheave bearings on mobile cranes, tower cranes and derricks shall be regularly lubricated according to the recommendations of the manufacturers or builders of such cranes or derricks.

(2) *Moving parts.* All moving parts of mobile cranes, tower cranes and derricks for which lubrication is specified, including ropes and chains, shall be regularly lubricated. Lubricating systems shall be frequently checked for proper delivery of the lubricant. Lubricating points shall be accessible without moving guards or other parts.

(m) *Operation near power lines.* The operation of any mobile crane, tower crane or derrick near or around any power line or power facility shall be done only in accordance with the provisions of subpart 23-1 of this Part (rule).

(n) *Use of mobile cranes in concrete work.* In building construction where concrete is raised by mobile cranes, such loads raised to elevations more than 150 feet shall be deposited or discharged only in hoppers or other appropriate facilities which are so located as to permit operation of the boom of any such crane at a minimum load radius.

23-8.2 Special provisions for mobile cranes. (a) *Inspection.* (1) A mobile crane which is moved from one job site to another without dismantling beyond the folding of the boom and such additional dismantling as may be necessary for that purpose is not required to be inspected before being first erected or operated on each job site to which it is moved, providing the monthly inspections are performed on schedule.

(2) The inspection and repair of mobile crane booms shall be made only when such booms are lowered and adequately supported.

(b) *Footings and outriggers.* (1) *Footings.* A firm footing shall be provided for every mobile crane. Where such firm footing is not naturally available, it shall be provided by substantial timbers, cribbing or other structural members sufficient to distribute the load so as not to exceed the safe bearing capacity of the underlying material.

(2) *Outriggers.* (i) Means shall be provided to hold all outriggers of mobile cranes in their retracted positions while such cranes are traveling and in their extended positions when blocked for hoisting.

[23-8.2]

(ii) Where used on mobile cranes, power-operated jacks shall be provided with means to prevent loss of jack support under load.

(iii) Each outrigger on a mobile crane shall be visible from its actuating location.

(iv) Means shall be provided to securely fasten outrigger floats to the outriggers when in use.

(c) *Hoisting the load.* (1) Before hoisting a load the person directing the lift shall see that the mobile crane is level and, where necessary, blocked.

(2) Before hoisting any load at a new job site, the boom of a mobile crane shall be test operated to its maximum height.

(3) Loads lifted by mobile cranes shall be raised vertically so as to avoid swinging during hoisting except when such operations are permitted by the capacity chart. A tag or restraint line shall be used when rotation or swinging of any load being hoisted by a mobile crane may create a hazard.

(4) When a mobile crane is operated at a fixed radius, the boomhoist pawl or other positive locking device shall be engaged.

(d) *Mobile crane travel.* (1) A mobile crane traveling to or from one job site to another or traveling on a street or highway shall not carry any jibs, attachments, buckets or other devices or material attached in any way to the boom whether the boom is in the folded position or not.

Exception: A hydraulic crane where the jib is permanently hinged to the boom or any crane where the manufacturer authorizes that the design of such crane guarantees the safe transport of the jib or other attachments.

(2) Mobile cranes shall not travel with suspended loads unless such crane is under the control of a competent, designated person who shall be responsible for the position of the load, boom location, ground support, travel route and speed of movement.

(3) A mobile crane, with or without load, shall not travel with the boom so high that it may bounce back over the cab.

(e) *Counterweights for mobile cranes.* Counterweights shall be provided for and used on mobile cranes as specified by the manufacturers or builders of such cranes or by professional engineers licensed to practice in the State. A mobile crane shall not be operated without the full amount of ballast or counterweight in place. Mobile cranes that do not have the ballast or counterweight attached may be operated temporarily with special care when handling light loads. The ballast or counterweight in place on any mobile crane shall not exceed the manufacturer's or builder's specifications.

(f) *Mobile crane construction.* (1) *Booms.* (i) Booms, boom sections and jibs of every mobile crane shall be constructed of suitable steel and shall be used only for the purposes recommended by the manufacturer or builder of such mobile crane.

(ii) The boom of any mobile crane shall not be raised from the level of the surface on which the crane rests other than by the use of its own hoisting capabilities. The design, construction and length of any boom shall be such that there is no undue stress imposed on the crane structure or mechanism during such raising operations.

(iii) Boom stops shall be provided on mobile cranes to prevent overtopping.

(iv) Any boom extension used on a mobile crane which is not provided by the manufacturer or builder of the crane shall be designed by a professional engineer licensed to practice in the State. A copy of the design plans for such boom extension shall be kept at the job site available for examination by the commissioner.

[23-8.2]

(2) *Braking mechanism.* In addition to the hoisting mechanism brakes required by this subpart, every mobile crane shall be provided with the following:

(i) An adequate braking mechanism for the boom hoist.

(ii) A swing lock or swing brake capable of preventing rotation.

(iii) A brake or other equivalent device adequate to bring the mobile crane to a stop from any travel for which such crane is designed, together with a means of locking such mobile crane so as to hold it stationary.

(3) *Boom sheave guard.* The sheave at the end of a mobile crane boom on which the hoisting rope operates shall be provided with a guard to prevent the rope from leaving the sheave in case of rope slack or any other condition.

(g) *Mobile crane capacity charts.* (1) *Load ratings for mobile cranes.*

(i) Load ratings shall not exceed the percentages listed in Table XVII of this subpart of the tipping loads for mobile cranes.

(ii) The stability of mobile cranes will be influenced by such factors as freely suspended loads, track, wind or ground conditions, condition and inflation of tires, boom lengths and proper operating speeds for existing conditions. All such factors shall be taken into account in determining mobile crane stability.

TABLE XVII
MAXIMUM LOAD RATINGS FOR MOBILE CRANES

Type of Mobile Crane Mounting	Maximum Load Ratings (Percentages of Tipping Loads)
Crawler without outriggers	75
Crawler, outriggers fully extended	85
Truck and wheel mounted (with or without outriggers fully extended)	85

(2) *Mobile crane capacity chart required.* (i) Every mobile crane shall be provided with a capacity chart which shall be posted and maintained clearly legible in the cab of the crane visible to the crane operator from his operating position. Such chart shall set forth the safe loads which may be hoisted by such crane at various lengths of boom at various boom angles and radial distances. Where outriggers are provided, such safe loads shall be set forth on the capacity chart with and without the use of the outriggers. Such chart shall also indicate whether or not such handling accessories as hooks, blocks and slings are included.

[23-8.2]

(ii) Unless furnished by the manufacturer or builder of the mobile crane, the required capacity chart shall be prepared and certified by a professional engineer licensed to practice in the State and a copy thereof submitted, on request, to the commissioner.

(iii) No load shall be lifted by any mobile crane that exceeds the relevant maximum specified by its capacity chart.

(h) Boom *angle indicator.* Every mobile crane having either a boom exceeding 40 feet in length or a maximum rated capacity exceeding 15 tons shall be provided with an approved boom angle indicator. Such boom angle indicator shall indicate the boom angle in degrees and shall be clearly visible to the mobile crane operator from his operating position at all times. Such boom angle indicator shall emit a visible or audible warning signal whenever the boom angle is unsafe.

Exception: Boom angle indicators are not required to be operative when such mobile cranes are used for excavation work with clamshells or dragline buckets.

(i) *Unauthorized operation.* The operator's cab of every mobile crane shall be kept locked whenever the operator is not present. No unauthorized person shall enter the cab of or remain immediately adjacent to any mobile crane in operation. Ignition locks, locking bars or other equivalent devices shall be provided to prevent unauthorized operation of mobile cranes.

(j) *Operation of a mobile crane with a demolition ball.* In addition to the general requirements of this Part (rule) for mechanical demolition, the operation of a mobile crane with a demolition ball shall be subject to the following provisions:

(1) The weight of any demolition ball shall not exceed 50 per cent of the safe load capacity of the boom length used at its lowest angle of operation.

(2) During operation with a demolition ball the swing of the boom shall not exceed 30 degrees from the center line, front to back, of the crane mounting.

(3) The windows of such crane cabs shall be constructed of shatterproof glass or shall be protected by adequate metal screens.

(4) The load line and the attachment of the demolition ball to the load line shall be inspected at least twice daily.

(5) Truck-mounted mobile cranes without outriggers shall not be used with a demolition ball.

23-8.3 Special provisions for tower cranes. (a) *Tower crane erection.* (1) Every tower crane used in construction shall be erected in accordance with the manufacturer's recommendations and under the supervision of a competent, designated person experienced in tower crane erection.

(2) Prior to the erection of any tower crane the ability of the supporting system, including slabs, foundations and the underlying soil to support the loads intended to be imposed thereon shall be certified by professional engineer licensed to practice in the State.

(3) Tower cranes shall be erected so that the jibs and counterweights can swing 360 degrees without striking any building, structure or any other object.

[23-8.3]

(4) Prior to initial use, a newly erected tower crane shall undergo a static overload test in the direction of least stability. Such test shall consist of suspending a load at the rated load and at the maximum radius for a period of at least one hour. Subsequent to such test, settlement of the equipment and load-bearing foundation shall be within the limits specified by the tower crane manufacturer. A written report of such test shall be kept on the job site available for examination by the commissioner.

(b) *Tower crane capacity chart.* Every tower crane shall be provided with a capacity chart which shall be posted and maintained legible in the cab of the crane clearly visible to the operator from his operating position. Where a remote control stand is used a duplicate of such capacity chart shall be affixed to such control stand. Such capacity chart shall be furnished by the manufacturer of the crane and shall include a full and complete range of crane load ratings at all stated operating radii for each allowable speed and for each recommended counterweight loading.

(c) *Tower crane construction.* (1) *Limit switches.* Limit switches which shall be sealed against unauthorized tampering shall be provided as follows:

(i) To limit trolley travel at either end of the jib.

(ii) To limit load block upward motion to prevent two-blocking.

(iii) To limit the load being lifted to no more than 110 per cent of the rated load upon completion of the static overload test as specified in paragraph 23-8.3(a) (4) of this section, above.

(2) *Cabs and remote control stations.* (i) Tower crane cabs and remote control stations for such cranes shall be protected from falling objects and material and from the elements.

(ii) Cab windows shall be constructed of transparent safety glazing material and shall provide clear visibility in all directions.

(iii) Cabs and remote control stations for tower cranes shall be heated to a temperature of at least 60 degrees Fahrenheit during cold weather whenever occupied.

(iv) Cabs and remote control stations for tower cranes shall be adequately ventilated.

(3) *Accessibility.* Adequate and safe means of access to and egress from the cabs and machinery platforms of tower cranes shall be provided. Where it is necessary to inspect the jib attachments located on the jib of any tower crane, a footwalk with suitable handrails shall be provided for such inspections.

(4) *Brakes.* In addition to the hoisting brakes required by this subpart, tower cranes shall be provided with the following:

(i) *Slewing brake.* Every tower crane shall be provided with a brake having adequate holding power in either direction to prevent movement of the jib when desired during normal crane operation. Such brake shall be capable of being set in the holding position and kept there without attention from the operator.

(ii) *Trolley brake.* The trolley of every tower crane shall be provided with an automatic brake or device capable of stopping movement of the trolley in case of trolley rope breakage.

(5) *Electrical equipment.* (i) *All* electrical equipment of tower cranes shall be grounded.

(ii) All tower cranes shall be provided with lightning protection.

(iii) All controls of tower cranes shall be of the deadman type.

(iv) In the event of power failure, all tower crane brakes shall be set automatically.

(6) *Climbing jacks.* Where climbing jacks are provided for tower cranes such jacks shall be equipped with over-pressure relief valves, pressure gages and check valves designed to retain pressure in case of hydraulic line failure.

[23-8.3]

(7) *Wind velocity device.* Every tower crane shall be provided with a device for measuring wind velocity. The sensing portion of every such device shall be mounted on the highest point of the crane while the readout of every such device shall be located in the cab or remote control station of the tower crane.

(8) *Counterweights.* Counterweights used on tower cranes shall be in accordance with the manufacturers' recommendations. Counterweights shall be securely fastened to the counter jib to prevent pieces from being accidentally dislodged.

(d) *Inspection and maintenance.* (1) Tower cranes shall be inspected and maintained in accordance with the manfacturers' recommendations.

(2) Where the mast of any tower crane runs through floor openings in the building or other structure in which the crane is mounted and the mast is secured by wedges or braces, such wedges or braces shall be inspected for tightness and dislocation at least twice each working day.

(e) *Operation of tower cranes.* (1) *Operators.* Tower cranes shall be operated only by persons who are qualified in accordance with the provisions of section 23-8.5 of this subpart.

(2) *Operation in windy conditions.* Tower cranes shall not be operated when the wind speed is at any time greater than 30 miles per hour. Tower cranes shall not be raised to new operating levels when the wind speed exceeds 20 miles per hour.

(3) Operation without counterweight prohibited. No tower crane shall be operated without the full amount of ballast or counterweight in place as specified by the manufacturer or builder of the crane or by a professional engineer licensed to practice in the State.

23-8.4 Special provisions for derricks. (a) *Bracing of foot blocks.* The foot blocks of every derrick shall be securely supported and firmly anchored against movement in any direction.

(b) *Guys.* (1) *Number and spacing.* The top of any guy derrick mast more than 25 feet in height shall be steadied by not less than six wire rope guys so spaced as to make the angles between adjacent guys approximately equal.

(2) *Attachment.* Wire rope guys shall be secured by either weldless steel sockets, thimble and splice connections, thimbles with proper size and numbers of rope clips or cast steel guy plates having grooved bearing surfaces of the same shape and size as the wire rope thimbles, using a spliced or wire rope clip attachment.

(3) *Anchoring.* Guys shall be attached to strong permanent con struction or to substantial "dead men" securely anchored in the ground.

(c) *Breast-type derricks.* Breast-type derricks shall be guyed from both the front and rear. Where front guys are not possible because of derrick operation, provisions shall be made to prevent such derricks from tipping over backward. Breast-type derricks which are operated by hand power shall have hand grips securely and positively fastened to the shaft and a ratchet and pawl shall be provided which will hold any load.

(d) *Derrick construction.* (1) *Materials.* The mast, boom, frame and similar parts of a derrick shall be constructed of suitable steel or of selected wood of proper strength and durability.

(2) *Mast fittings.* On derricks which have booms larger than the masts, the gudgeon pins, mast tops and goosenecks shall be securely fastened to the tops of the masts to prevent such parts from pulling out when the booms are raised.

(e) *Derrick capacity charts.* (1) A capacity chart shall be provided for every derrick and such chart shall be posted conspicuously on the job site. Unless furnished by the manufacturer or builder of the derrick, the capacity chart shall be prepared and certified by a professional engineer licensed to practice in the State and a copy thereof shall be submitted, upon request, to the commissioner.

[23-8.4]

(2) A derrick shall not lift any load that exceeds the relevant maximum specified on its capacity chart.

(f) *Derrick boom raising.* The boom of any derrick shall not be raised from the level of the surface on which the derrick rests other than by the use of its own hoisting capabilities. The design, construction and length of the boom shall be such that there is no undue stress imposed on the derrick structure or mechanism during such raising operations.

23-8.5 Special provisions for crane operators. (a) *Finding of fact.* The board finds that the trade or occupation of operating cranes of the type described in subdivision (b) of this section, in construction, demolition and excavation work involves such elements of danger to the lives, health and safety of persons employed in such trade or occupation as to require special regulations for their protection and for the protection of other employees and the public in that such cranes may fall over, collapse, contact electric power lines, dislodge material and cause such material to fall or fail to support intended loads and convey them safely, unless such cranes are operated by persons of proper ability, judgment and diligence.

(b) *Limited application of this section.* This section applies only to mobile cranes having a manufacturers' maximum rated capacity exceeding five tons or a boom exceeding forty feet in length and to all tower cranes operating in construction, demolition and excavation work. The word crane as used in this section refers to tower cranes and to such mobile cranes of the following type: a mobile, carrier-mounted, power operated hoisting machine utilizing hoisting rope and a power-operated boom which moves laterally by rotation of the machine on the carrier.

(c) *Certificate of competence required.* No person, whether the owner, or otherwise, shall operate a crane in the State, unless such person is a certified crane operator by reason of the fact that:

(1) he holds a valid certificate of competence issued by the commissioner to operate a crane; or

(2) he is at least 21 years of age and holds a valid license issued by the Federal government, a State government or by any political subdivision of this or any other State and such license has been accepted in writing by the commissioner as equivalent to a certificate of competence issued by him; or

(3) he is a person who:

(i) is at least 21 years of age and is employed by the Federal government, the State or a political subdivision, agency or authority of the State and is operating a crane owned or leased by the Federal government the State or such political subdivision, agency or authority and h5 assigned duties include operation of a crane;

(ii) is at least 21 years of age and is employed only to test or repair a crane and is operating it for such purpose while under the direct supervision of a certified crane operator; or under the direct supervision of a person employed by the Federal government, the State or a political subdivision, agency or authority of the State and his assigned duties include the operation of a crane;

(iii) an apprentice or learner who is at least 18 years of age and who has the permission of the owner or lessee of a crane to take instruction in its operation and is operating such crane under the direct supervision of a certified crane operator or under the direct supervision of a person employed by the Federal government, the State or a political subdivision agency or authority of the State and whose assigned duties include the operation of a crane.

[23-8.5]

(d) *Application forms and photographs.* An application for a certificate of competence or for a renewal thereof shall be made on forms provided by the commissioner. Upon notice from the commissioner to an applicant that a certificate of competence or a renewal thereof will be issued to him, the applicant must forward photographs of himself in such numbers and sizes as the commissioner shall prescribe, and such photographs must have been taken within 30 days of the request for such photographs.

(e) *Physical conditions.* No person suffering from a physical handicap or illness, such as epilepsy, heart disease, or an uncorrected defect in vision or hearing, that might diminish his competence, shall be certified by the commissioner.

(f) *Experience required.* An applicant for a certificate of competence must be at least 21 years of age and must have had practical experience in the operation of cranes for at least three years and, in addition, have a practical knowledge of crane maintenance.

(g) *Examining board.* The commissioner may appoint an examining board which shall consist of at least three members, at least one of whom shall be a crane operator who holds a valid certificate of competence issued by the commissioner, and at least one of whom shall be a representative of crane owners. The members of the examining board shall serve at the pleasure of the commissioner and their duties will include:

(1) The examination of applicants and their qualifications, and the making of recommendations to the commissioner with respect to the experience and competence of the applicants.

(2) The holding of hearings regarding appeals following denials of certificates.

(3) The holding of hearings prior to determinations of the commissioner to suspend or revoke certificates, or to refuse to issue renewals of certificates.

(4) The reporting of findings and recommendations to the commissioner with respect to such hearings.

(5) The acts and proceedings of the examining board shall be in accordance with regulations issued by the commissioner.

(h) *General examination.* Each applicant for a certificate of competence will, and each applicant for a renewal thereof may, be required by the commissioner to take an appropriate general examination.

(i) *Operating examination.* An applicant who passes the general examination will also be required to take a practical examination in crane operation, except that the commissioner may waive this requirement with respect to an applicant for a renewal of a certificate of competence.

(j) *Contents of certificate.* Each certificate of competence issued shall include the name and address of the certified crane operator, a brief description of him for the purpose of identification and his photograph.

(k) *Term of certificate.* Each certificate of competence or renewal thereof shall be valid for three years from the date issued, unless its term is extended by the commissioner or unless it is sooner suspended or revoked. The commissioner may extend the term of any certificate of competence as he may find necessary to relieve a certified operator of unnecessary hardship.

(l) *Carrying certificate.* Each certified crane operator shall carry his certificate on his person when operating any crane and failure to produce the certificate upon request by the commissioner shall be presumptive evidence that the operator is not certified.

(m) *Renewals.* An application for renewal of a crane operator's certificate of competence shall be made within one year from the expiration date of the certificate sought to be renewed, except that the commissioner may extend the time to make such application to prevent any undue hardship to a certified crane operator.

[23-8.5]

(n) *Suspension, revocation, refusal to renew, denials of certificates, hearings.* (1) The commissioner may, upon notice to the interested parties and after a hearing before the examining board, suspend or revoke a certificateof competence upon finding that the certified operator has failed to comply with an order of the commissioner or that the certified operator is not a person of proper competence, judgment or ability in relation to the operation of cranes, or for other good cause shown.

(2) Prior to a determination by the commissioner not to renew a certificate of competence, the commissioner shall require a hearing before the examining board upon notice to the interested parties.

(3) (i) An applicant whose application for a certificate has been denied by the commissioner may, upon his written request made to the commissioner within 30 days after the mailing or personal delivery to him of a notice of such denial, have a hearing before the examining board.

(ii) Such hearing shall be held by the examining board which shall make its recommendations to the commissioner within three days after such hearing has been concluded. A written notice of the commissioner's decision, containing the reasons therefor, shall be promptly given to the certified operator or applicant, as the case may be, and to any interested parties who appeared at the hearing. Every such hearing shall be held in accordance with such regulations as the commissioner may establish.

POWER-OPERATED EQUIPMENT

23-9.1 Application of this subpart. The provisions of this subpart shall apply to power-operated heavy equipment or machinery used in construction, demolition and excavation operations. These provisions shall not apply to material or personnel hoists, (see subpart 23-6) nor to cranes and derricks (see subpart 23-8).

23-9.2 General requirements. (a) *Maintenance.* All power-operated equipment shall be maintained in good repair and in proper operating condition at all times. Sufficient inspections of adequate frequency shall be made of such equipment to insure such maintenance. Upon discovery, any structural defect or unsafe condition in such equipment shall be corrected by necessary repairs or replacement. The servicing and repair of such equipment shall be performed by or under the supervision of designated persons. Any servicing or repairing of such equipment shall be performed only while such equipment is at rest.

(b) *Operation.* (1) All power-operated equipment used in construction, demolition or excavation operations shall be operated only by trained, designated persons and all such equipment shall be operated in a safe manner at all times.

(2) Operators of power-operated material handling equipment shall remain at the controls while any load is being handled.

(c) *Loading.* Power-operated material handling equipment shall not be loaded in excess of the manufacturer's design live load rating. All loads shall be properly trimmed to prevent dislodgment of any part of such loads during transit.

(d) *Protection of moving parts.* Gears, belts, sprockets, drums, sheaves and any points of contact between moving parts of power-operated equipment or machines when not guarded by location shall be guarded in compliance with this Part (rule) and with Industrial Code Part (Rule No.) 19.

(e) *Refueling.* While refueling, the engines of power-operated equipment or machines shall be stopped except for turbo-charged diesel engines which are refueled through a special connection which prevents exposure of the fuel to the atmosphere. Open flames and any spark producing devices shall be kept a safe distance away from any area where engines are being refueled. Persons shall not smoke or carry lighted smoking materials in such area.

(f) *Engine exhaust.* Steam or exhaust gases from power-operated equipment shall be discharged at a point where such steam or gases will not contaminate the air in a working zone. Such discharges shall be in compliance with any regulations, orders, or laws promulgated by any authority concerned with air pollution.

(g) *Equipment at rest.* The operators of material handling equipment shall not leave such equipment while loads, buckets or blades are suspended. Any such load, bucket or blade shall be brought to rest on blocks, shall be lowered to the ground, grade or equivalent surface or shall be brought to the lowest end of travel of the equipment.

(h) *Roll-over protection required.* (1) Roll-over protective structure.

(i) Any new self-propelled earth-moving, excavating or grading equipment or machines, whether mounted on crawlers or wheels, which is sold or offered for sale in the State after January 1, 1973 shall be equipped with an approved roll-over protective structure when such equipment is used or intended to be used at any location in the State subject to the provisions of the Labor Law or of this Part (rule). Such equipment shall include: grader; bulldozer; tractor (prime mover) having a manufacturer's rated flywheel horsepower of 50 or more; front end loader with bucket capacity rated by the manufacturer at one cubic yard or more; scraper and off-highway type hauler having capacities rated by the manufacturers at five cubic yards or more.

[23-9.2]

(ii) Any self-propelled earth-moving, excavating or grading equipment or machines, whether mounted on crawlers or wheels, which has been manufactured after July 1, 1971 and before December 31, 1972, and which is sold or offered for sale in the State, shall be equipped with an approved roll-over protective structure by July 1, 1973, when such equipment is used or intended to be used at any location in the State subject to the provisions of the Labor Law or of this Part (rule).

(iii) Such roll-over protective structure shall be designed, constructed and installed to protect the operator in the event of accidental overturning of such equipment.

(2) *Approved seat belt required.* Any equipment required by this Part (rule) to have an approved roll-over protective structure shall also be provided with an approved seat belt for each seat. Such seat belt shall be used by the operator whenever the equipment is being operated.

Exception: Tractors with pipe-laying equipment installed are not required to be provided with the roll-over protection.

(i) *Riding.* Persons shall not ride on the loads, buckets, blades, slings, balls, hooks, or similar parts of power-equipped equipment or machines.

23-9.3 Conveyors and cableways. (a) *Walkways.* Walkways along and adjacent to conveyor belts shall be kept free of materials and shall be unobstructed for their entire length. Where such walkways are located three feet or more above the ground, grade, floor or equivalent surface such walkways shall be provided with a safety railing constructed and installed in compliance with this Part (rule).

(b) *Trippers.* Where trippers are used to control discharge of materials from conveyors devices for throwing the belt drives into neutral shall be installed at both ends of the runways.

(c) *Spillage.* Where conveyor belts cross over any sidewalk, street, highway, or any other area where persons may work or pass, trays of sufficient size to catch any spillage from such belts shall be installed.

(d) *Overhead protection.* Where persons work or pass directly beneath a conveyor, overhead protection in compliance with this Part (rule) shall be provided.

(e) *Signal system required.* A signal system in compliance with subpart 23-6 of this Part (rule) shall be used in conjunction with conveyors for starting and stopping and for the raising and lowering of loads.

(f) *Riding prohibited.* No person shall ride any conveyor belt or the bucket or load handled by any cableway.

23-9.4 Power shovels and backhoes used for material handling. Where power shovels and backhoes are used for material handling, such equipment and the use thereof shall be in accordance with the following provisions:

(a) *Strength.* Such equipment shall be so constructed, placed and operated as to be stable. Such equipment shall not be stressed beyond their capacities as determined by the manufacturers.

(b) *Inspection.* (1) Such equipment shall be thoroughly inspected by designated persons at intervals not exceeding three months.

(2) Inspection and repair of each such machine shall be performed with the motor stopped and with the boom lowered and adequately supported.

[23-9.4]

(3) A written, dated record of the most recent inspection of each such machine shall be made on a form supplied by the commissioner and shall be signed by the designated person making such inspection. Such written record shall be kept on the job site available for examination by the commissioner.

(c) *Footing.* Firm, level and stable footing shall be provided for each such machine. Where such footing is not otherwise supplied, it shall be provided by substantial timbers, cribbing or other structural members in sufficient numbers and of sufficient size to distribute the load so as not to exceed the safe bearing capacity of the underlying material.

(d) *Hoisting mechanism brakes and locking devices.* (1) Such equipment shall be provided with brakes or equivalent devices capable of sustaining at rest one and one-half times the maximum rated load.

(2) Hand- or foot-operated brakes or equivalent devices shall be provided with substantial locking mechanisms to lock such brakes or equivalent devices while they are engaged.

(e) *Attachment of load.* (1) Any load handled by such equipment shall be suspended from the bucket or bucket arm by means of wire rope having a safety factor of four.

(2) Such wire rope shall be connected by means of either a closed shackle or a safety hook capable of holding at least four times the intended load.

(f) *Limitation on modifications.* No modifications affecting the load handling capacity of such machines shall be made unless the modification is certified by either the manufacturer of the equipment or by a professional engineer licensed to practice in the State.

(g) *Capacity.* No load shall be lifted by such equipment that exceeds the maximum load specified by the manufacturer of such equipment.

(h) *General operation.* (1) Any load lifted by such equipment shall be raised in a vertical plane to minimize swing during hoisting.

(2) Such equipment shall not travel with a suspended load except on surfaces which conform to the requirements of subdivision (c) of section 23-9.4 of this Part (rule).

(3) Ignition locks or equivalent means shall be provided to prevent unauthorized use of such equipment.

(4) Unauthorized persons shall not be permitted in the cab or immediately adjacent to any such equipment in operation.

(5) Carrying or swinging suspended loads over areas where persons are working or passing is prohibited.

(6) Operation near power lines or power facilities shall be in compliance with this Part (rule).

23-9.5 Excavating machines. (a) *Footing.* Excavating machines shall not be used where unstable conditions or slopes of the ground or grade may cause such machines to tilt dangerously. To prevent such unstable conditions, mats of timber or equivalent means to afford stable footings shall be provided.

(b) *Protection of operator.* Where an operator of an excavating machine may be exposed to an overhead hazard, such equipment shall be provided with a cab or equivalent cover affording protection against such hazard.

[23-9.5]

(c) *Operation.* Excavating machines shall be operated only by designated persons. No person except the operating crew shall be permitted on an excavating machine while it is in motion or operation. No person other than the pitman and excavating crew shall be permitted to stand within range of the back of a power shovel or within range of the swing of the dipper bucket while the shovel is in operation. When an excavating machine is not in use, the blade or dipper bucket shall rest on the ground or grade. The operator of an excavating machine shall not leave the controls of such machine at any time when the master clutch is engaged and the engine is operating. Oiling and greasing shall be performed only while an excavating machine is at rest and the master clutch disengaged. The boom or the bucket, dipper or clamshell of a power shovel shall not pass over the seat or cab of a truck or other vehicle while any person is in such seat or cab.

(d) *Operation near power lines or power facilities.* The operation of excavating machines near power lines or power facilities shall be in compliance with this Part (rule).

(e) *Trenching.* Material shall not be pushed manually into the path of trenching machines.

(f) *Stopping or parking excavating machines.* The operator of any excavating machine shall not leave the controls of such machine until he has lowered the bucket or blade into firm contact with the ground or grade surface.

(g) *Backing.* Every mobile power-operated excavating machine except for crawler-mounted equipment shall be provided with an approved warning device so installed as to automatically sound a warning signal when such machine is backing. Such warning signal shall be audible to all persons in the vicinity of the machine above the general noise level in the area.

23-9.6 Aerial baskets. (a) *Equipment inspection.* Prior to the use of an aerial basket the operator shall make a daily inspection of the equipment.

(1) Such daily inspection shall include the following:

(i) All attachment welds between the actuating cylinders and the boom or pedestal.

(ii) All pivot pins for security of their locking devices.

(iii) All exposed ropes, sheaves and leveling devices for both excessive wear and security of attachment.

(iv) Hydraulic systems for leaks and excessive wear.

(v) Boom and basket for cracks and abrasions.

(vi) The lubrication and fluid levels.

(2) A test operation of the boom from the ground controls through one complete cycle shall be performed by the operator. The basket controls shall be tested to make sure that they are in proper working order. The truck driver shall test the truck brakes and other automotive operating accessories.

(3) A record of such inspection and testing which may affect the safe operation of the aerial basket shall be corrected before such aerial basket is placed in operation.

(b) *Aerial basket safeguards.* (1) Where aerial basket controls are so located that they may come into contact with obstructions, such controls shall be protected by guarding or equivalent protection shall be provided.

(2) The lower controls at ground or grade level shall be capable of overriding the controls located in the basket.

(c) *Driving or moving of aerial basket truck.* (1) Aerial basket truck drivers an aerial basket operators shall be competent designated persons who have been trained in the operation and use of such equipment.

[23-9.6]

    (2) The instrument panel of the truck cab shall be equipped with an automatic warning device, such as a light or similar device, to warn the driver when the boom is raised.

    (3) Driving or moving the aerial basket truck while any person is elevated in the basket is prohibited.

(d) *Truck placement.* Prior to aerial basket operation, the truck shall be placed only on solid ground or equivalent surface to provide a substantially sound footing for the truck wheels and outriggers. The truck shall be so located that both front and rear axles are approximately horizontal, though they may be at different elevations, so that the truck does not lean sideways. Before the operation of the basket, a person stationed on the ground shall, by signaling the truck driver, position the truck and maneuver the empty basket into the proper working position. The basket shall then be returned to the ground or cradled in its traveling position. Such person shall also examine the outriggers for proper positioning and truck stability. Before such outriggers are lowered or extended, such person shall make sure that no obstructions or other persons are in the way.

(e) *Aerial basket operation.* (1) The use of an aerial basket as an anchoring point for a block and tackle, or as a make-shift boom on a straight lift is prohibited.

    (2) Aerial basket equipment designed for use as a derrick shall be equipped with an approved boom angle indicator so that the operator will know the boom angle at all times. A capacity chart showing safe loads, boom heights and horizontal reach distances at various boom angles shall be installed next to the operating controls clearly legible to the operator from his operating position.

    (3) Before the basket is moved, the operator shall observe the location of all obstructions and any other hazards which may be in the vicinity. The operator shall always face the direction in which the basket is moving or is about to move.

    (4) The operation of an aerial basket near power lines or power facilities shall be in compliance with this Part (rule).

    (5) All air or oil supply hoses for power tools used from the aerial basket shall be free of any conductive material.

    (6) The truck and the aerial basket vehicle shall be adequately grounded at all times when in use or the basket shall be isolated from the truck by insulation.

    (7) Where aerial baskets are operated near power lines and power facilities, materials and tools shall not be passed between a person on the ground or grade level and a person in the basket, unless both such persons are wearing high-voltage rubber gloves and other protective equipment, such as rubber sleeves and safety hats or caps. During such use of an aerial basket, persons shall not enter or leave the truck while the boom or basket is near or in contact with electrically energized equipment and no person on the ground or grade level shall be suffered or permitted to touch the truck.

    (8) Persons shall enter or leave an aerial basket only when such basket is resting on the ground or grade level or cradled in the traveling position. Persons shall stand clear of the path of the basket and boom when such basket is being lowered. Any movement of the vehicle while persons are elevated in the basket is prohibited.

    (9) While persons are in the elevated basket, persons on the ground or grade level shall not enter the area directly beneath such basket except when required by the persons in the basket.

    (10) Tools, equipment and materials shall not be thrown from or to the elevated basket.

    (11) All tools not in use shall be adequately secured in trays in the baskets, or adequately secured in suitable belt holsters.

    (12) Standing on the rim of the basket, placing and standing on boards across the rim of the basket or placing and standing on ladders in the basket is prohibited.

[23-9.6]

(13) Unless in an emergency situation, or upon request of a person in the aerial basket, the controls to lower the boom shall be operated only by persons in the elevated basket.

23-9.7 Motor trucks. (a) *Brake maintenance.* The brakes of every motor truck shall be so maintained that such truck with full load may be securely held on any grade that may be encountered in normal use on the job.

(b) *Blocks.* (1) Provision shall be made to apply wheel blocks to any truck ascending any ramp with a slope steeper than one in 10 to prevent the truck from sliding in case of stall.

(2) No person shall work under the raised body of a dump truck unless such body is securely blocked to prevent accidental lowering.

(c) *Loading.* Trucks shall not be loaded beyond their rated capacities and all loads shall be trimmed before the trucks are moved. Loads that are apt to become dislodged in transit shall be securely lashed in place.

(d) *Backing.* Trucks shall not be backed or dumped in places where persons are working nor backed into hazardous locations unless guided by a person so stationed that he sees the truck drivers and the spaces in back of the vehicles.

(e) *Riding.* No person shall be suffered or permitted to ride on running boards, fenders or elsewhere on a truck or similar vehicle except where a properly constructed and installed seat or platform is provided.

(f) *Dumping.* No person shall be located within the body (load carrying portion) of a truck while the dumping mechanism is being operated.

(g) *Cab protector.* Dump steel bodies which are loaded by mechanical means shall be equipped with suitable steel cab protectors which cover at least the rear quarter of the tops of such cabs.

23-9.8 Lift and fork trucks. (a) *Capacity.* A metal plate with legible etched or stamped figures giving the capacity rating in pounds shall be attached to every lift or fork truck. A pouch firmly secured to the truck and containing a document having the following information may be used as a means of identifying the load rating of the truck: truck make, model, serial number, and load rating in pounds.

(b) *Overloading prohibited.* No lift or fork truck shall be loaded beyond its capacity rating.

(c) *Brakes and load-elevating mechanisms.* Every power-operated fork and lift truck shall be provided with a lockable brake. The load-elevating mechanism shall be capable of being locked at any elevation.

(d) *Hand-lift handles.* Every pallet truck having a hand-lift handle shall be provided with an automatic device to retain the raised load and free the handle until it is re-engaged by the operator.

(e) *Operating surfaces.* No lift or fork truck shall be used on any surface that is so uneven as to make upsetting likely.

(f) *Packaged masonry units.* No masonry units packaged by means of wire or metal tape shall be handled by a lift or fork truck when any part of such wire or tape binding is broken.

(g) *Loose masonry units.* Unless palletized masonry units are securely bound in package form, provisions shall be made to prevent spillage.

(h) *Support of pallets.* Loaded pallets shall be kept level at all times. Masonry units used as pallet supports shall be securely lashed to the pallet and shall be of proper quality and number to provide stable footing for the load. Loose material and other unstable supports for pallets shall not be used.

(i) *Protection of operator.* Every fork lift truck shall be provided with a substantial overhead canopy or screen to protect the operator from falling objects and materials

[23-9.8]

(j) *Prohibited use.* No lift or fork truck shall be in motion when the loaded forks are elevated higher than necessary to clear floor obstructions except as required for positioning to deposit the load.

(k) *Riding on forks.* No person shall stand or ride on the forks of a moving fork lift truck.

(1) *Warning devices.* Every power-operated fork lift truck shall be equipped with a horn, whistle, gong or similar warning device which can be actuated by the operator. Such device shall be clearly audible above the normal noise level in the work area.

23.9.9 Power buggies. (a) *Assigned operator.* No person other than a trained and competent operator designated by the employer shall operate a power buggy.

(b) *Defective machines.* No power buggy shall be operated unless it is in compliance with this Part (rule) and is in good operating condition.

(c) *Mechanical requirements.* (1) *Stability.* Every power buggy shall be so designed and constructed as to withstand without tilting the following:

(i) A 45 degree turn at full rated load and maximum designed forward speed.

(ii) A collision stop against wheel blockage on a level grade at full rated load and one-half maximum designed forward or full reverse speed.

(iii) Lateral traversal of 10 per cent grade slopes at full rated load and maximum designed speed.

(2) *Braking power.* (i) Every power buggy shall be provided with brakes and tire surfaces capable of bringing such buggy to a full stop within 25 feet on a level dry plank surface or frictional equivalent at full rated load and maximum designed speed.

(ii) Brakes shall be capable of being fixed in engagement to hold the full load stationary on a 25 per cent grade.

(3) *Accidental starting.* The controls of every power buggy shall be so arranged, shielded or located that they cannot be accidentally engaged.

(4) *Warning devices.* Every power buggy except those having maximum speeds of three miles per hour and upon which no person rides shall be equipped with an easily operable horn or other audible warning signal. Such audible horn or other signal shall be capable of being heard above the normal noise level in the area.

(5) *Seats and visibility.* Every power buggy of the riding type shall be provided with an operator's seat or standing platform designed and secured to prevent slipping off and so located that the operator may have maximum practicable driving visibility.

(6) *Speed.* Every power buggy of the riding type shall be designed or equipped so that it cannot travel faster than 12 miles per hour on a level surface.

(d) *Operation.* (1) *Parking on grades.* No power buggy shall be left unattended on any grade sufficiently steep to cause such buggy to coast if free of engine and brake resistance.

(2) *Prohibited operation.* No power buggy shall be operated:

(i) at a speed greater than 12 miles per hour;

(ii) when carrying more than its full rated load;

(iii) on insecure or slippery surfaces or on surfaces so inclined or uneven as to endanger stability;

(iv) on grades steeper than 25 per cent; or

(v) on ramps, runways or other surfaces not in compliance with this Part (rule).

(e) *Special requirements for runways and ramps.* Runways, ramps, platforms and other surfaces upon which power buggies are operated shall conform to the following requirements:

(1) They shall be substantially constructed and securely supported, braced and fastened to prevent movement.

[23-9.9]

(2) They shall be constructed to sustain without failure at least four times the maximum load for which they are intended.

(3) The minimum width inside of curbs for any ramp, runway or platform for single lane power buggy traffic shall be two feet wider than the outside width of any power buggy operated thereon and two feet wider than twice such buggy width in places where passing or two lane traffic occurs.

(4) Ramps shall be limited to maximum grades of one on four.

(5) All runways shall be substantially level transversely.

(6) Curbs in compliance with this Part (rule) shall be provided along the edges of surfaces upon which power buggies are operated as follows:

(i) Curbs shall be furnished along all edges which are nearer than 10 feet horizontally to the edge of any unenclosed floor area, shaft or other open space into or through which a fall from such surface of more than 24 inches vertically is possible, except as set forth in subparagraph (iii) below.

(ii) Where curbs are not required because the buggy is operated on a surface not over 24 inches above any floor or equivalent surface below, such lower surface shall be strong enough to sustain the loaded power buggy in event of a fall thereon.

(iii) Curbs may be omitted at actual dumping points more than 24 inches above any floor or equivalent surface below if the edge over which the dumping occurs is provided with bumpers or other means which will effectively stop the buggy from running over the edge while dumping.

23-9.10 Pile drivers. (a) *Footing.* Before placing or advancing a pile driver, the ground shall be inspected and, where necessary for firm and level footing, cribbing or timber mats shall be provided to assure stability for the pile driver. After placing or advancing a pile driver, inspection and correction of the footing shall be made as necessary to maintain such stability.

(b) *Inspection.* All pile driving equipment shall be inspected daily before the start of work and every defect or unsafe condition shall be immediately corrected before pile driving operations are begun.

(c) *Protection of operator.* The operator of every pile driver shall be protected from falling objects or materials, steam, cinders and water by a substantial covering.

(d) *Qualifications of operators.* Each member of the pile driving crew shall be properly instructed in the work he is to perform and the pile driving operation shall be in charge of a trained, designated person who alone shall direct the work and give the operating signals.

(e) *Handling of piles.* The preparation of the piles shall be done at a safe distance from the driving operation. During the hoisting of piles, all persons not actually engaged in operating the equipment and handling the piles shall be kept from the area.

(f) *When not in use.* When any pile driver is not in use the hammer shall be chocked or blocked in the leads or lowered to the ground or grade level.

(g) *Temporary interruption.* The operator of every pile driver shall remain at the controls when the driving is interrupted until the hammer has been chocked or blocked in the leads, or has been lowered and is resting on a driven pile or on the ground.

(h) *Steam and air lines.* Steam and air hose shall be securely fastened in place at couplings and intermediate points to prevent dangerous whipping of such hose in the event of a break. The control valves for steam and air lines shall be located within easy reach of the operator at his operating position.

(i) *Driving plates, cushions and striking heads.* Driving plates, cushions and striking heads shall be securely and positively fastened in such manner as to prevent their dislodgment during the driving operations

[23-9.10]

(j) *Ladders.* A ladder extending from the bottom of the leads to the overhead sheaves shall be permanently attached to the structure supporting the leads.

(k) *Working platforms.* Where a structural tower supports the leads, working platforms consisting of planking at least two inches thick, full size, laid tight shall be provided on all levels of the leads at which it is necessary for persons to work. Such platforms shall be provided with safety railings constructed and installed in compliance with this Part (rule) on all sides, except on the hammer or lead side of the platforms. Where such platforms cannot be provided approved safety belts and lifelines shall be provided.

(1) *Mandril support.* Mandrils shall be attached to the leads by safety chains or cables to prevent dislodging or falling during connection to piles.

23-9.11 Mixing machines. (a) *Charging skips.* Each time before raising or lowering a charging skip, the operator shall make sure that no person is located in the danger area. In addition, there shall be a safety railing constructed and installed in compliance with this Part (rule) on both sides of the charging skip so arranged as to prevent passage of any person under the raised skip.

(b) *Hoppers.* Hoppers into which a person may fall shall be effectively guarded with a substantial iron grating consisting of crossbars of one-half inch round stock or its equivalent, spaced not to exceed five inches between bars. Maximum openings in such grating shall be one square foot in size.

(c) *Bucket hoists.* Where a falling hazard exists at the point where a mixer discharges into a bucket hoist, such point shall be guarded by location, by a safety railing constructed and installed in compliance with this Part (rule) or by other equivalent means.

(d) *Flywheels.* Flywheels and power transmission mechanisms shall be kept covered and guarded against accidental contact.

(e) *Trough type mixers.* The revolving blades of trough or batch type mixing machines shall be guarded with a substantial iron grating consisting of crossbars of one-half inch round stock or its equivalent, spaced not to exceed five inches between bars and located at least five inches above the blades.

BASIC FUNDAMENTALS OF GEARS

CONTENTS

		Page
I.	Types of Gears	1
II.	The Bevel Gear	2
III.	The Worm and Worm Wheel	3
IV.	Changing Direction with Gears	4
V.	Changing Speed	5
VI.	Magnifying Force with Gears	6
VII.	Summary	7

BASIC FUNDAMENTALS OF GEARS

Did you ever take a clock apart to see what made it tick? Of course you came out with some parts left over when you got it back together again. And they probably included a few gear wheels. Gears are used in many machines. Frequently the gears are hidden from view in a protective case filled with grease or oil, and you may not see them.

An egg beater gives you a simple demonstration of the three things that gears do. They can change the direction of motion; increase or decrease the speed of the applied motion; and magnify or reduce the force which you apply. Gears also give you a positive drive. There can be, and usually is, creep or slip in a belt drive. But gear teeth are always in mesh, and there can be no creep and slip.

Follow the directional changes in figure 1. The crank handle is turned in the direction indicated by the arrow-clockwise, when viewed from the right. The 32 teeth on the large vertical wheel A mesh with the 8 teeth on the right-hand horizontal wheel B, which rotates as indicated by the arrow. Notice that as B turns in a clockwise direction, its teeth mesh with those of wheel C and cause wheel C to revolve in the opposite direction. The rotation of the crank handle has been transmitted by gears to the beater blades, which also rotate.

Now figure out how the gears change the speed of motion. There are 32 teeth on gear A and 8 teeth on gear B. But the gears mesh, so that one complete revolution of A results in four complete revolutions of gear B. And since gears B and C have the same number of teeth, one revolution of B results in one revolution of C. Thus the blades revolve four times as fast as the crank handle.

Previously you learned that third-class levers increase speed at the expense of force. The same thing happens with this egg beater. The magnitude of the force is changed. The force required to turn the handle is greater than the force applied to the frosting by the blades. Therefore a mechanical advantage of less than one results.

I. TYPES OF GEARS

When two shafts are not lying in .the same straight line, but are parallel, motion can be transmitted from one to the other by means of spur gears. This setup is shown in figure 2.

Spur gears are wheels with mating teeth cut in their surfaces so that one can turn the other without slippage. When the mating teeth are cut so that they are parallel to the axis of rotation, as shown in figure 2, the gears are called straight spur gears.

When two gears of unequal size are meshed together, the smaller of the two is usually called a pinion. By unequal size, we mean an unequal number of teeth causing one gear to be of a larger diameter than the other. The teeth, themselves, must be of the same size in order to mesh properly.

The most commonly used type are the straight spur gears, but quite often you'll run across another type of spur gear called the helical spur gear.

In helical gears the teeth are cut slantwise across the working face of the gear. One end of the tooth, therefore, lies ahead of the other. In other words, each tooth has a leading end and a trailing end. A look at these gears in figure 3A will show you how they're constructed.

In the straight spur gears the whole width of the teeth comes in contact at the same time. But with helical (spiral) gears contact between two teeth starts first at the leading ends and moves progressively across the gear faces until the trailing ends are in contact. This kind of meshing action keeps the gears in constant contact with one another. Therefore, less lost motion and

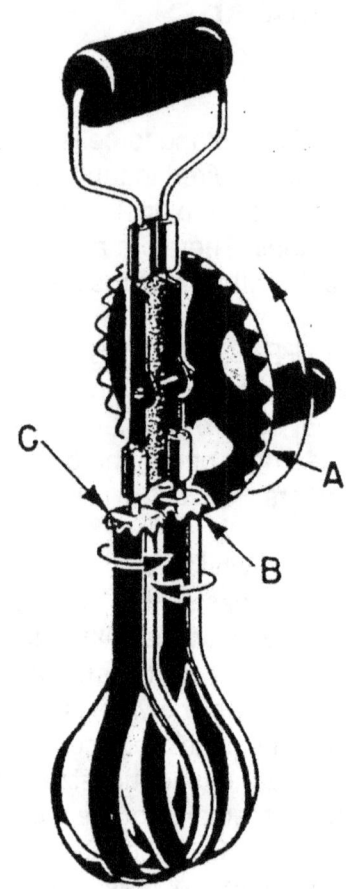

Figure 1.—A simple gear arrangement.

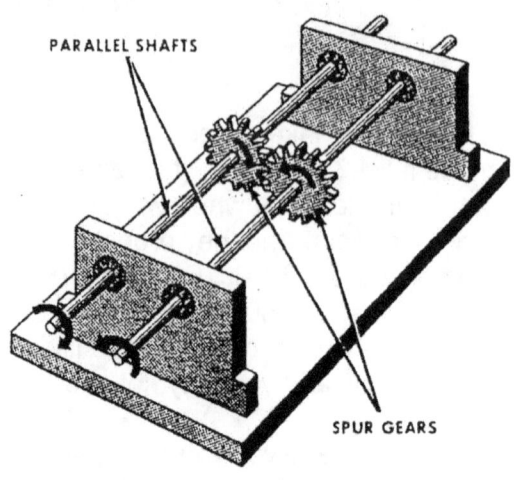

Figure 2.—Spur gears coupling two parallel shafts.

smoother, quieter action is possible. One disadvantage of this helical spur gear is the tendency of each gear to thrust or push axially on its shaft. It is necessary to put a special thrust bearing at the end of the shaft to counteract this thrust.

Thrust bearings are not needed if herringbone gears like those shown in figure 4 are used. Since the teeth on each half of the gear are cut in opposite directions, each half of the gear develops a thrust which counterbalances that of the other half. You'll find herringbone gears used mostly on heavy machinery.

Figure 3 also shows you three other gear arrangements in common use.

The internal gear in figure 3B has teeth on the inside of a ring, pointing inward toward the axis of rotation. An internal gear is always meshed with an external gear, or pinion, whose center is offset from the center of the internal gear. Either the internal or pinion gear can be the driver gear, and the gear ratio is calculated the same as for other gears-by counting teeth.

Often only a portion of a gear is needed where the motion of the pinion is limited. In this case the sector gear (fig. 3C) is used to save space and material. The rack and pinion in figure 3D are both spur gears. The rack may be considered as a piece cut from a gear with an extremely large radius. The rack-and-pinion arrangement is useful in changing rotary motion into linear motion.

II. THE BEVEL GEAR.-So far most of the gears you've learned about transmit motion between parallel shafts. But when shafts are not parallel (at an angle), another type of gear is usedthe bevel gear. This type of gear can connect shafts lying at any given angle because they can be beveled to suit the angle.

Figure 5A shows a special case of the bevel gear-the miter gear. A pair of miter gears is used to connect shafts having a 90 angle, which means the gear faces are beveled at a 45° angle.

You can see in figure 5B how bevel gears are designed to join shafts at any angle. Gears cut at any angle other than 45 are called just plain bevel gears.

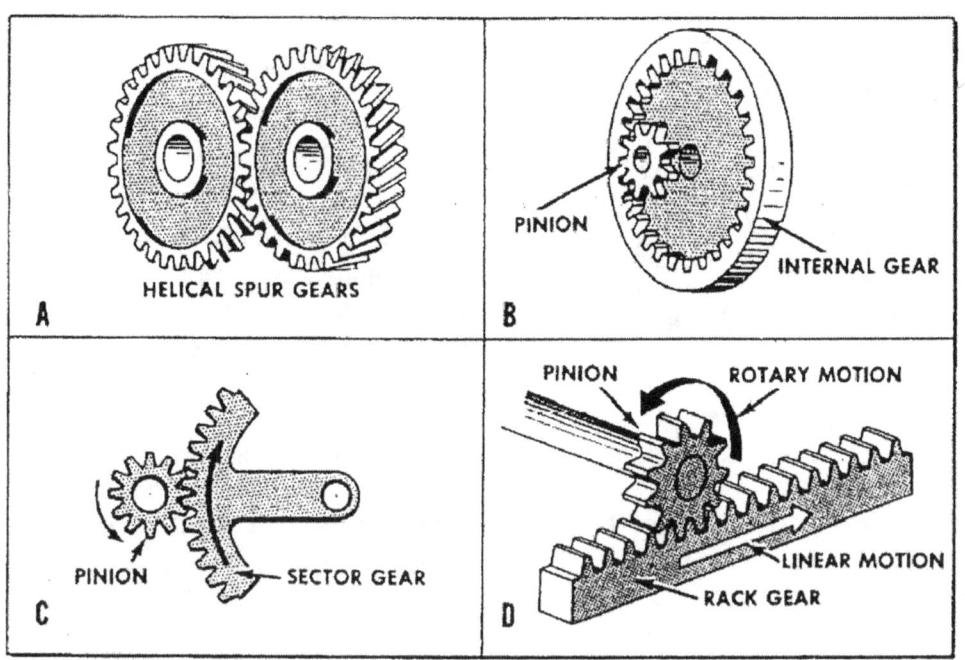

Figure 3.—Gear types.

The gears shown in figure 5 are called straight bevel gears, because the whole width of each tooth comes in contact with the mating tooth at the same time. However, you'll also run across spiral bevel gears with teeth cut so as to have advanced and trailing ends. Figure 6 shows you what spiral bevel gears look like. They have the same advantages as other spiral (helical) gearsless lost motion and smoother, quieter operation.

III. THE WORM AND WORM WHEEL.-Worm and worm-wheel combinations, like those in figure 7, have many uses and advantages. But it's better to understand their operating theory before learning of their uses and advantages.

Figure 7A shows the action of a single-thread worm. For each revolution of the worm, the worm wheel turns one tooth.

Figure 4.—Herringbone gear.

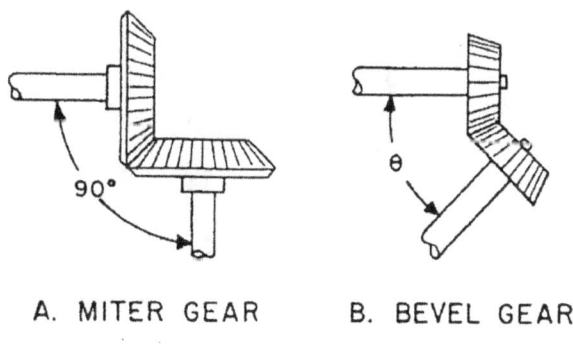

A. MITER GEAR B. BEVEL GEAR

Figure 5.—Bevel gears.

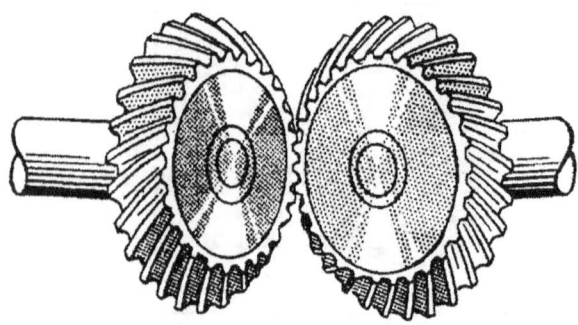

Figure 6 — Spiral bevel gears.

Thus if the worm wheel has 25 teeth the gear ratio is 25:1.

Figure 7B shows a double-thread worm. For each revolution of the worm in this case, the worm wheel turns two teeth. That makes the gear ratio 25:2 if the worm wheel has 25 teeth.

Likewise, a triple-threaded worm would turn the worm wheel three teeth per revolution of the worm.

A worm gear is really a combination of a screw and a spur gear. Tremendous mechanical advantages can be obtained with this arrangement. Worm drives can also be designed so that only the worm is the driver the spur cannot drive the worm. On a hoist, for example, you can raise or lower the load by pulling on the chain which turns the worm. But if you let go of the chain, the load cannot drive the spur gear and let the load drop to the deck. This is a non-reversing worm drive.

IV. CHANGING DIRECTION WITH GEARS

No doubt you know that the crankshaft in an automobile engine can turn in only one direction. If you want the car to go backwards, the effect of the engine's rotation must be reversed. This is done by a reversing gear in the transmission, not by reversing the direction in which the crankshaft turns.

A study of figure 8 will show you how gears are used to change the direction of motion. This is a schematic diagram of the sight mounts on a Navy gun. If you crank the range-adjusting handle A in a clockwise direction the gear B directly above it is made to rotate in a counterclockwise direction. This motion causes the two pinions C and D on the shaft to turn in the same direction as gear B against the teeth cut in the bottom of the table. The table is tipped in the direction indicated by the arrow.

As you turn the deflection-adjusting handle E in a clockwise direction the gear F directly above it turns in the opposite direction. Since the two bevel gears G and H are fixed on the shaft with F, they also turn.

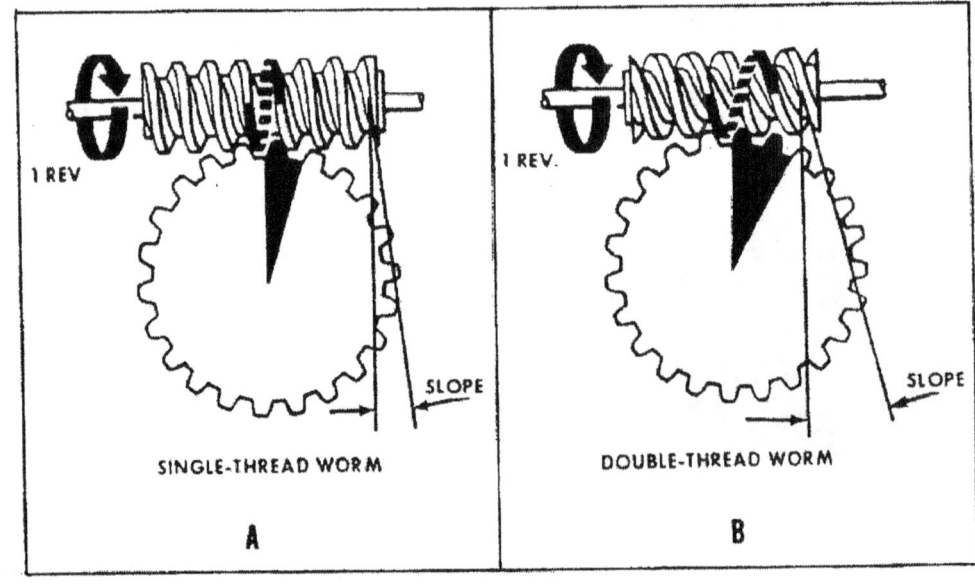

Figure 7. — Worm gears.

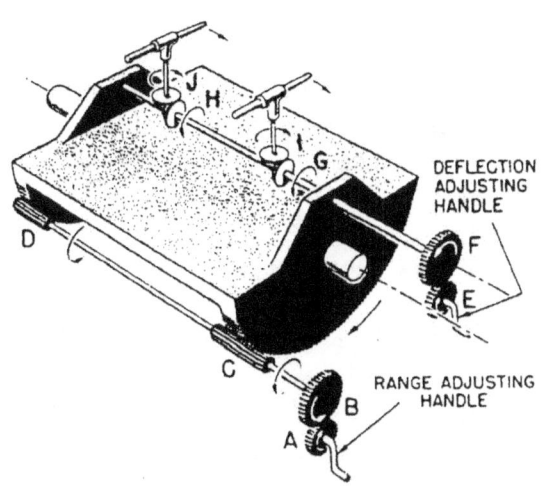

Figure 8.—Gears change direction of applied motion.

These bevel gears, meshing with the horizontal bevel gears I and J, cause I and J to swing the front ends of the telescopes to the right. Thus with a simple system of gears, it is possible to keep the two telescopes pointed at a moving target. In this and many other practical applications, gears serve one purpose—to change the direction of motion.

V. CHANGING SPEED

As you've already seen in the eggbeater, gears can be used to change the speed of motion. Another example of this use of gears is found in your clock or watch. The mainspring slowly unwinds and causes the hour hand to make one revolution in 12 hours. Through a series—or train—of gears, the minute hand makes one revolution each hour, while the second hand goes around once per minute.

Figure 6-9 will help you to understand how speed changes are made possible. Wheel A has 10 teeth which mesh with the 40 teeth on wheel B. Wheel A will have to rotate four times to cause B to make one revolution. Wheel C is rigidly fixed on the same shaft with B. Thus C makes the same number of revolutions as B. However, C has 20 teeth, and meshes with wheel D which has only 10 teeth. Hence, wheel D turns twice as fast as wheel C.

Now, if you turn A at a speed of four revolutions per second, B will be rotated at one revolution per second. Wheel C also moves at one revolution per second, and causes D to turn at two revolutions per second. You get out two revolutions per second after having put in four revolutions per second. Thus the overall speed reduction is 2/4 or 1/2, which means that you got half the speed out of the last driven wheel that you put into the first driver wheel.

You can solve any gear speed-reduction problem with this formula

$$S_2 = S_1 \times \frac{T_1}{T_2}$$

where
S_1 = speed of first shaft in train
S_2 = speed of last shaft in train
T_1 = product of teeth on all drivers
T_2 = product of teeth on all driven-gears

Now use the formula on the gear train of figure 6-8.

$$S_2 = S_1 = \times \frac{T_1}{T_2} = 4 \times \frac{10 \times 20}{40 \times 10} =$$

$$\frac{800}{400} = 2 \, revs. \, per \, sec.$$

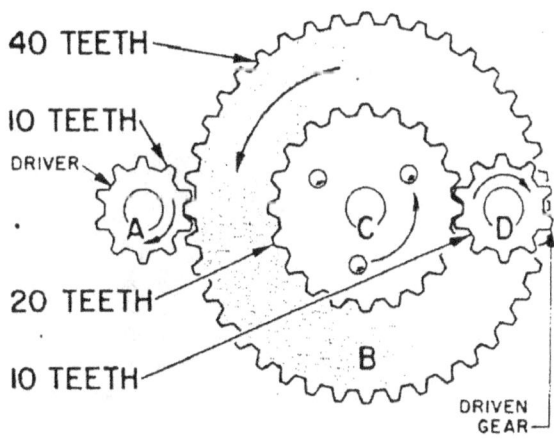

Figure 9.—Gears can change speed of applied motion.

Almost any increase or decrease in speed can be obtained by choosing the correct gears for the job. For example, the turbines on a ship have to turn at high speeds-say 5800 rpm-if they are going to be efficient. But the propellers, or screws, must turn rather slowly say 195 rpm-to push the ship ahead with maximum efficiency. So, a set of reduction gears is placed between the turbines and the propeller shaft.

When two external gears mesh, they rotate in opposite directions. Often you'll want to avoid this. Put a third gear, called an idler, between the driver and the driven gear. But don't let this extra gear confuse you on speeds. Just neglect the idler entirely. It doesn't change the gear ratio at all, and the formula still applies. The idler merely makes the driver and its driven gear turn in the same direction. Figure 10 will show you how this works.

VI. MAGNIFYING FORCE WITH GEARS

Gear trains are used to increase the mechanical advantage. In fact, wherever there is a speed reduction, the effect of the effort you apply is multiplied. Look at the cable winch in figure 11. The crank arm is 30 inches long, and the drum on which the cable is wound has a 15-inch radius. The small pinion gear has 10 teeth, which mesh with the 60 teeth on the internal spur gear. You will find it easier to figure the mechanical advantage of this machine if you think of it as two machines.

First, figure out what the gear and pinion do for you. The theoretical mechanical advantage of any arrangement of two meshed gears can be found by the following formula

$$\text{M. A. (theoretical)} = \frac{T_o}{T_a}$$

In which, T_o = number of teeth on driven gear;
T_a = number of teeth on drive gear.
In this case, T_o =60 and T_a =10. Then,

$$\text{M. A. (theoretical)} = \frac{T_o}{T_a} = \frac{60}{10} = 6$$

Now, for the other part of the machine, which is a simple wheel-and-axle arrangement consisting of the crank arm and the drum. The theoretical mechanical advantage of this can be found by dividing the distance the effort moves $2\pi R$ in making one complete revolution, by the distance the cable is drawn up in one revolution of the drum - $2\pi r$.

$$\text{M. A. (theoretical)} = \frac{2\pi R}{2\pi r} = \frac{R}{r} = \frac{30}{15} = 2$$

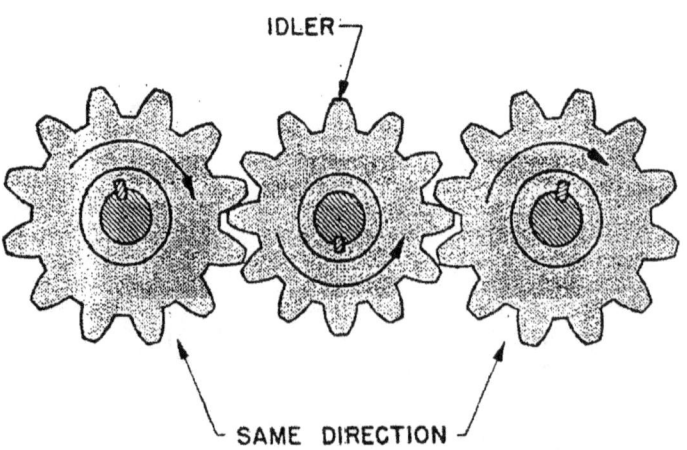

Figure 10.—An idler gear.

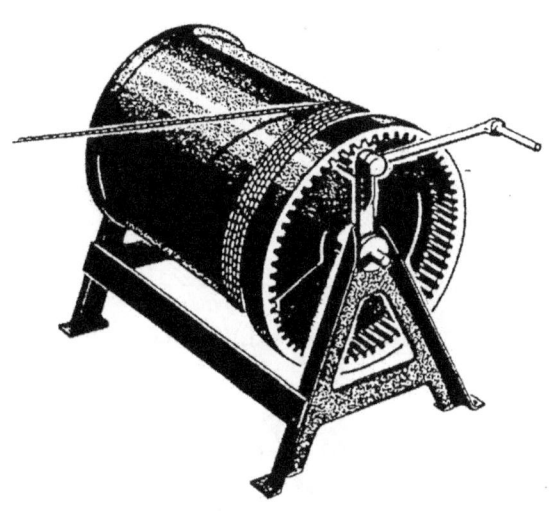

Figure 11.—This magnifies your effort.

You know that the total, or overall, theoretical mechanical advantage of a compound machine is equal to the product of the mechanical advantages of the several simple machines that make it up. In this case you considered the winch as being two machines—one having an M. A. of 6, and the other an M. A. of 2. Therefore, the over-all theoretical mechanical advantage of the winch is 6 x 2, or 12. Since friction is always present, the actual mechanical advantage may be only 7 or 8. Even so, by applying a force of 100 pounds on the handle, you could lift a load of 700 or 800 pounds.

You use gears to produce circular motion. But you often want to change rotary motion into up-and-down or linear motion. You can use cams to do this. For example-

The cam shaft in figure 12 is turned by the gear. A cam is keyed to the shaft and turns with it. The cam has an irregular shape which is designed to move the valve stem up and down, giving the valve a straight-line motion as the cam shaft rotates.

When the cam shaft rotates, the high point-lobe-of the cam raises the valve to its open position. As the shaft continues to rotate, the high point of the cam is passed and the valve is lowered to closed position.

A set of cams, two to a cylinder, driven by timing gears from the crankshaft operate the exhaust and intake valves on the gasoline automobile engine as shown in figure 13. Cams are widely used in machine tools and other devices to make rotating gears and shafts do up-and-down work.

VII. SUMMARY

These are the important points you should keep in mind about gears-
- Gears can do a job for you by changing the direction, speed, or size of the force which you apply.
- When two external gears mesh, they always turn in opposite directions. You can make them turn in the same direction by placing an idler gear between the two.
- The product of the number of teeth on each of the driver gears, divided by the product of the number of teeth on each of the driven gears, gives you the speed ratio of any gear train.
- The theoretical mechanical advantage of any gear train is the product of the number of teeth on the driven gear wheels, divided by the product of the number of teeth on the driver gears.
- The overall theoretical mechanical advantage of a compound machine is equal to the product of the theoretical mechanical advantages of all the simple machines which make it up.
- Cams are used to change rotary motion into linear motion.

One of the gear systems you'll get to see frequently aboard ship is that on the anchor winch. Figure 14 shows you one type in which you can readily see how the wheels go 'round. The driving gear A is turned by the winch engine or motor. This gear has 22 teeth, which mesh with the 88 teeth on the large wheel B. Thus, you know that the large wheel makes one revolution for every four revolutions of the driving gear A. You get a 4-to-1 theoretical mechanical advantage out of that pair. Secured to the same shaft with B is the small spur gear C, covered up here. The gear C has 30 teeth which mesh with the 90

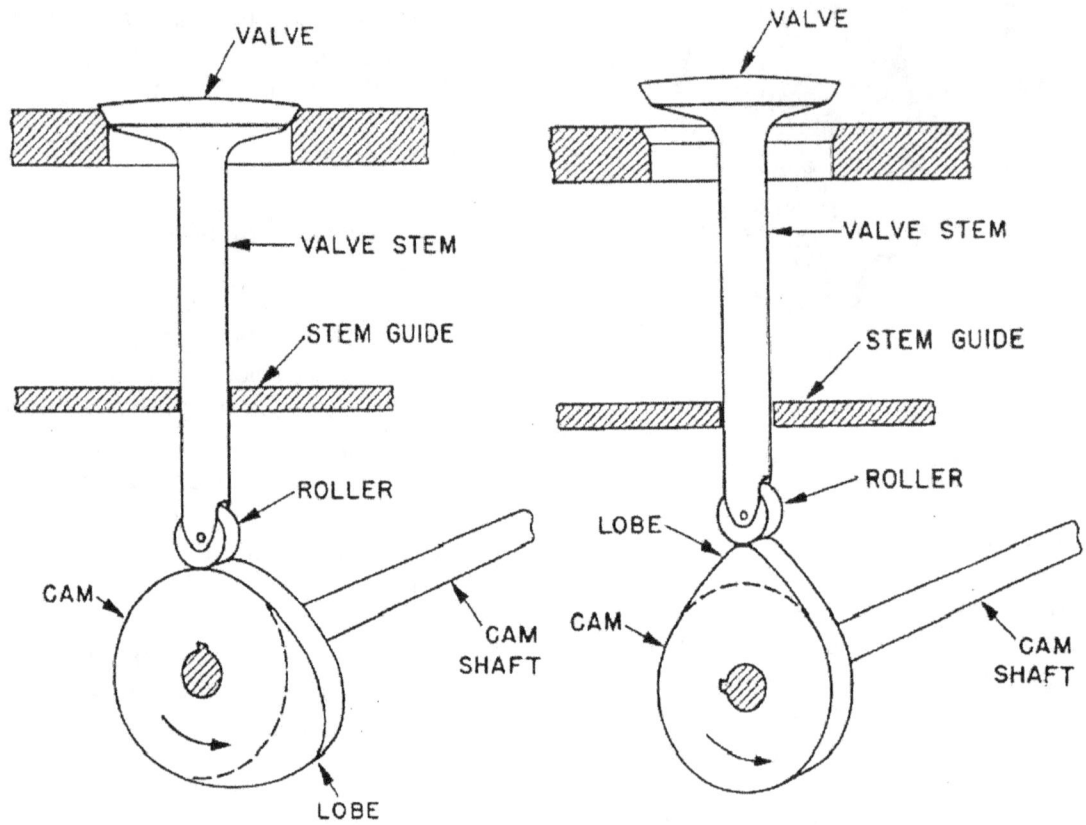

Figure 12.—Cam-driven valve.

teeth on the large gear D, also covered up. The advantage from C to D is 3 to 1.

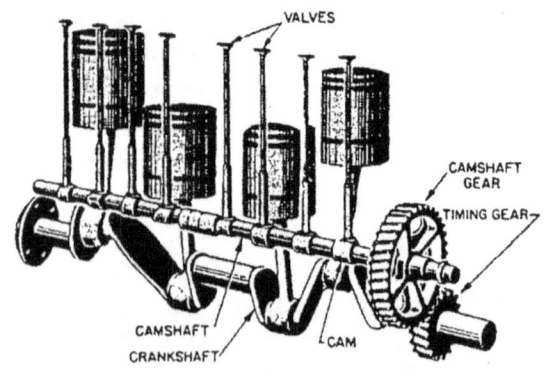

Figure 13.—Automobile valve gear.

The sprocket wheel to the far left, on the same shaft with D, is called a wildcat. The anchor chain is drawn up over this. Every second link is caught and held by the protruding teeth of the wildcat. The overall mechanical advantage of the winch is 4 x 3, or 12 to 1.

Figure 15 shows you an application of the rack and pinion as a steering mechanism. Turning the ship's wheel turns the small pinion A. This pinion causes the internal spur gear to turn. Notice that there is a large mechanical advantage in the arrangement.

Now you see that center pinion P turns. It meshes with the two vertical racks. When the wheel is turned full to the right, one rack moves downward and the other moves upward to the positions of the racks. Attached to the bottom of the racks are two hydraulic pistons which control the steering of the ship. You'll get some information on this hydraulic system in a later chapter.

Figure 14.—An anchor winch.

Figure 15.—A steering mechanism.

BASIC FUNDAMENTALS OF BLOCK AND TACKLE

Remember how your mouth hung open as you watched movers taking a piano out of a fourth story window? The fat guy on the end of the tackle eased the piano safely to the sidewalk with a mysterious arrangement of blocks and ropes. Or perhaps you've been in the country and watched the farmer use a block-and-tackle to put hay in a barn. Since old Dobbin or the tractor did the hauling, there was no need for a fancy arrangement of ropes and blocks. Incidentally, you'll often hear the rope or tackle called the fall. Block-and-tackle, or block-and-fall.

You will rig a block-and-tackle to make some of your work easier. Learn the names of the parts of a block. Figure 1 will give you a good start on this. Look at the single block and see some of the ways you can use it. If you lash a single block to a fixed object—an overhead, a yardarm, or a bulkhead—you give yourself the advantage of being able to pull from a convenient direction. For example, in figure 2 you haul up a flag hoist, but you really pull down. You can do this by having a single sheaved block made fast to the yardarm. This makes it possible for you to stand in a convenient place near the flag bag and do the job. Otherwise you would have to go aloft, dragging the flag hoist behind you.

I. MECHANICAL ADVANTAGE

With a single fixed sheave, the force of your down-pull on the fall must be equal to the weight of the object being hoisted. You can't use this rig to lift a heavy load or resistance with a small effort-you can change only the direction of your pull.

A single fixed block is really a first-class lever with equal arms. The arms EF and FR in figure 3 are equal; hence the mechanical advantage is one. When you pull down at A with a force of one pound, you raise a load of one pound at B. A single fixed block does not magnify force nor speed.

You can, however, use a single block-and-fall to magnify the force you exert.

Notice, in figure 4 that the block is not fixed, and that the fall is doubled as it supports the 200-pound cask. When rigged this way, a single block-and-fall is called a runner. Each half of the fall carries one half of the total load, or 100 pounds. Thus, by the use of the runner, the bluejacket is lifting a 200-pound cask with a 100-pound pull. The mechanical

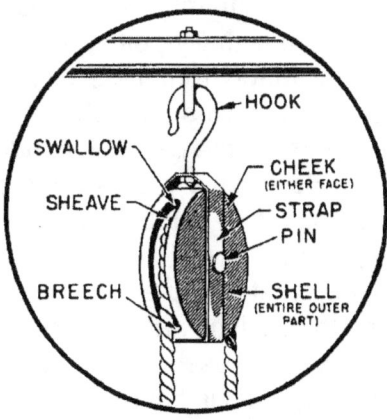

Figure 1.—Look it over.

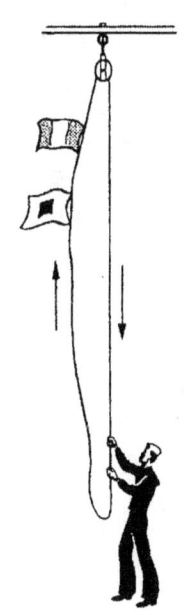

Figure 2 —A flag hoist.

advantage is two. Check this by the formula:

$$\text{M.A.} = \frac{R}{E} = \frac{200}{100}, \text{ or } 2$$

The single movable block in this setup is really a second-class lever. See figure 2-5. Your effort E acts upward upon the arm EF, which is the diameter of the sheave. The resistance R acts downward on the arm FR, which is the radius of the sheave. Since the diameter is twice the radius, the mechanical advantage is two.

But, when the effort at E moves up two feet, the load at R is raised only one foot. That's one thing to remember about blocks and falls-if you are actually getting a mechanical advantage from the system, the length of rope that passes through your hands is greater than the distance that the load is raised. However, if you can lift a big load with a small effort, you don't care how much rope you have to pull.

The bluejacket in figure 4 is in an awkward position to pull. If he had another single block handy, he could use it to change the direction of the pull, as in figure 6. This second arrangement is known as a guntackle purchase. Because the second block is fixed, it merely changes the direction of pull-and the mechanical advantage of the whole system remains two.

You can arrange blocks in a number of ways, depending on the job to be done and the mechanical advantage you want to get. For example, a luff tackle consists of a double block and a single block, rigged as in figure 7. Notice that the weight is suspended by the three parts of rope which extend from the movable single block. Each part of the rope carries its share of the load. If the crate weighs 600 pounds, then each of the three parts of the rope supports its share 200 pounds. If there's a pull of 200 pounds downward on rope B, you will have to pull downward

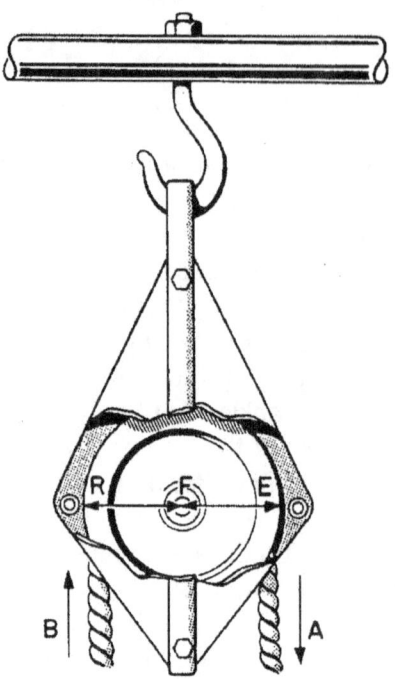

Figure 3.—No advantage.

with a force of 200 pounds on A to counterbalance the pull on B. Neglecting the friction in the block, a pull of 200 pounds is all that is necessary to raise the crate. The mechanical advantage is:

$$\text{M.A.} = \frac{R}{E} = \frac{600}{200} = 3$$

Here's a good tip. If you count the number of the parts of rope going to and from the movable block, you can figure the mechanical advantage at a glance. This simple rule will help you to quickly approximate the mechanical advantage of most tackles you see.

Many combinations of single, double, and triple sheave blocks are possible. Two of these combinations are shown in figure 8.

If you can secure the dead end of the fall to the movable block, the advantage is increased by one. Notice that this is done in figure 7. That is a good point to remember. Don't forget, either, that the strength of your fall-rope-is a limiting factor in any tackle. Be sure your fall will carry the load. There is no point in rigging a six-fold purchase which carries a 5-ton load with two triple blocks on a 3-inch manila rope attached to a winch.

The winch could take it, but the rope couldn't.

Now for a review of the points you have learned about blocks, and then to some practical applications-

With a single fixed block the only advantage is the change of direction of the pull. The mechanical advantage is still one.

A single movable block gives a mechanical advantage of two.

Many combinations of single, double, and triple blocks can be rigged to give greater advantages.

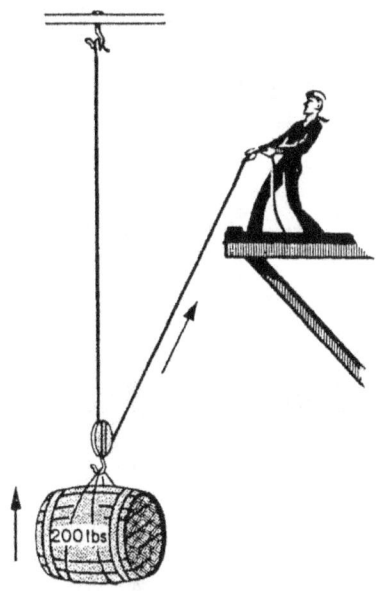

Figure 4.—A runner.

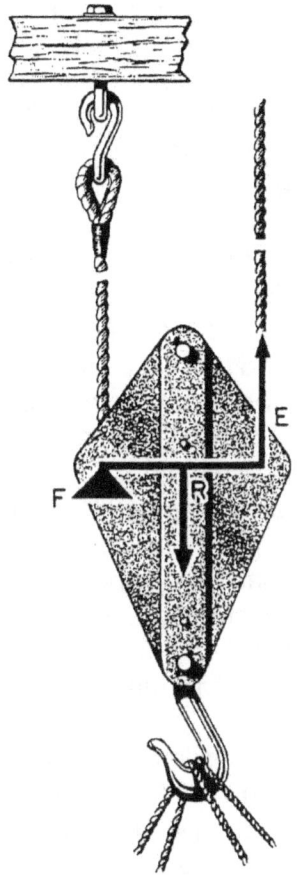

Figure 5.—It's 2 to 1.

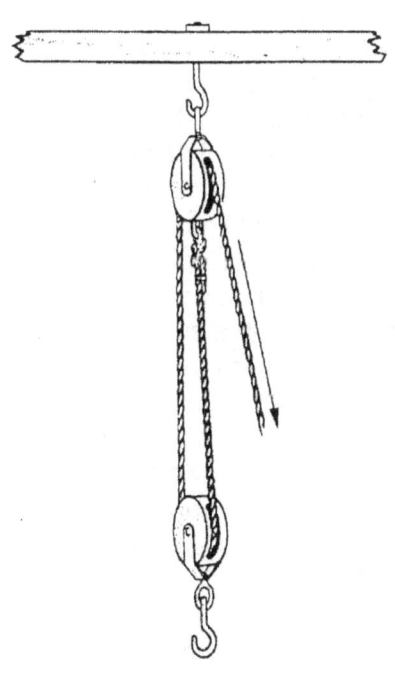

Figure 6.—A gun tackle.

A general rule of thumb is that the number of the parts of the fall going to and from the movable block tells you the approximate mechanical advantage of that tackle.

If you fix the dead end of the fall to the movable block you increase the mechanical advantage by one.

II. APPLICATIONS AFLOAT AND ASHORE

Blocks and tackle are used for a great number of lifting and moving jobs afloat and ashore. The five or six basic combinations are used over and over again in many situations. Cargo is loaded aboard, depth charges are placed in their racks, life boats are lowered over the side by the use of this machine. Heavy machinery, guns, and gun mounts are swung into position with the aid of blocks and tackle. In a thousand situations, bluejackets find this machine useful and efficient.

Yard and stay tackles are used on shipboard when you want to pick up a load from the hold and swing it onto the deck, or to shift any load a short distance. Figure 9 shows you how the load is first picked up by the yard tackle. The stay tackle is left slack. After the load is raised to the height necessary to clear obstructions, you take up on the stay tackle, and ease off on the yard fall. A glance at the rig tells you that the mechanical advantage of each of these tackles is only two. You may think that it isn't worth the trouble to rig a yard and stay tackle with that small advantage just to move a 400-pound crate along the deck. However, a few minutes spent in rigging may save many unpleasant hours with a sprained back.

If you want a high mechanical advantage, a luff upon luff is a good rig for you. You can raise heavy loads with this setup. Figure 10 shows you how it is rigged. If you apply the rule by which you count the parts of the fall going to and from the movable blocks, you find that block A gives a mechanical advantage of 3 to 1. Block B has four parts of fall running to and from it, a

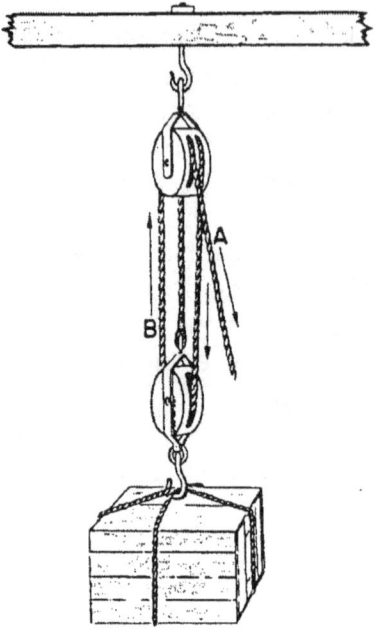

Figure 7.—A luff tackle.

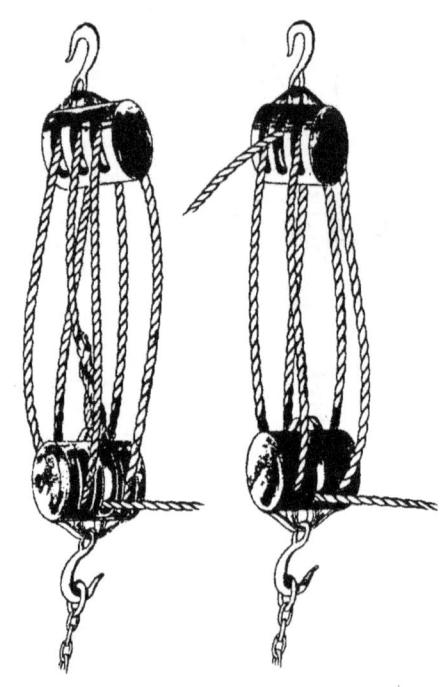

Figure 8.—Some other tackles.

mechanical advantage of 4 to 1. The mechanical advantage of those obtained from A is multiplied four times in B. The overall mechanical advantage of a luff upon luff is the product of the two mechanical advantages or 12.

Don't make the mistake of adding mechanical advantages. Always multiply them.

You can easily figure out the M.A. for the apparatus shown in figure 2-10. Suppose the load weighs 1,200 pounds. Since it is supported by the parts 1, 2, and 3 of the fall running to and from block A, each part must be supporting one third of the load, or 400 pounds. If part 3 has a pull of 400 pounds on it, part 4 which is made fast to block B, also has a 400-pound pull on it. There are four parts of the second fall going to and from block B, and each of these takes an

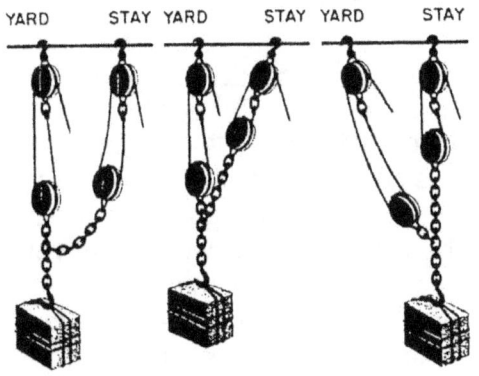

Figure 9.—A yard and stay tackle.

equal part of the 400-pound pull. Therefore, the hauling part requires a pull of only 1/4 x 400, or 100 pounds. So, here you have a 100-pound pull raising a 1,200-pound load. That's a mechanical advantage of 12.

In shops ashore and aboard ship you are almost certain to run into a chain hoist, or differential pulley. Ordinarily, these hoists are suspended from overhead trolleys, and are used to lift heavy objects and move them from one part of the shop to another.

To help you to understand the operation of a chain hoist, look at the one in figure 11. Assume that you grasp the chain at E and pull until the large wheel A has turned around once. Then the distance through which your effort has moved is equal to the circumference of that wheel, or $2\pi R$. How much will the lower wheel C and its load be raised? Since wheel C is a single movable block, its center will be raised only one-half the distance that the chain E was pulled, or a distance πR. However, the smaller wheel B, which is rigidly fixed to A, makes one revolution at the same time as A does so B will feed some chain down to C. The length of the chain fed down will be equal to the circumference of B, or $2\pi r$. Again, since C is single movable block, the downward movement of its center will be equal to only one-half the length of the chain fed to it, or πr.

Of course, C does not first move up a distance πR and then move down a distance πr. Actually, its steady movement upward is equal to the difference between the two,

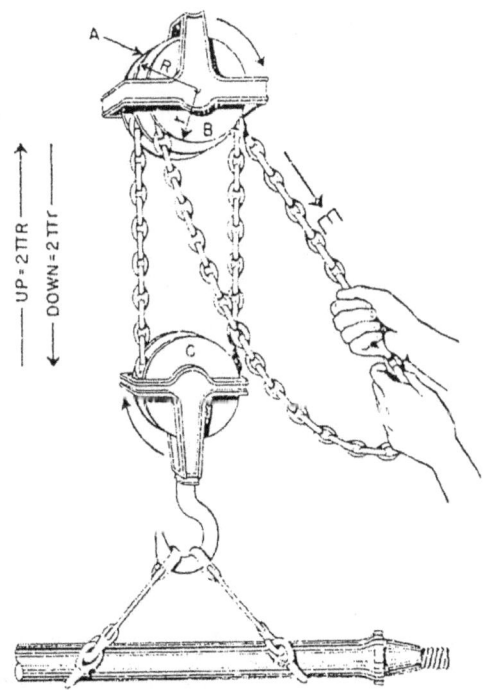

Figure 11.—A chain hoist.

or $(\pi R - \pi r)$. Don't worry about the size of the movable pulley, C. It doesn't enter into these calculations. Usually its diameter is between that of A and that of B.

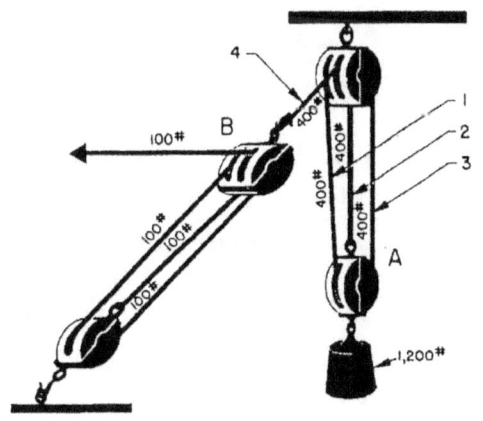

Figure 10.—Luff upon luff.

The mechanical advantage equals the distance through which the effort E is moved, divided by the distance that the load is moved. This is called the velocity ratio, or theoretical mechanical advantage. It is theoretical because the frictional resistance to the movement of mechanical parts is left out. In practical uses, all moving parts have frictional resistance.

The equation for theoretical mechanical advantage may be written-

Theoretical mechanical advantage =

$$\frac{\text{Distance effort moves}}{\text{Distance resistance moves}}$$

and in this case,

$$\text{T.M.A.} = \frac{2\pi R}{\pi R - \pi r} = \frac{2R}{(R-r)}$$

If A is a large wheel, and B is a little smaller, the value of 2R becomes large, and (R-r) becomes small. Then you have a large number for $\frac{2R}{(R-r)}$ which is the theoretical mechanical advantage.

You can lift heavy loads with chain hoists. To give you an idea of the mechanical advantage of a chain hoist, suppose the large wheel has a radius R of 6 inches and the smaller wheel a radius r of 5 3/4 inches. What theoretical mechanical advantage would you get? Use the formula-

$$\text{T.M.A.} = \frac{2R}{R-r}$$

Then substitute the numbers in their proper places, and solve-

$$\text{T.M.A.} = \frac{2 \times 6}{6 - 5\ 3/4} = \frac{12}{1/4} = 48$$

Since the friction in this type of machine is considerable, the actual mechanical advantage is not as high as the theoretical mechanical advantage would lead you to believe. For example, that theoretical mechanical advantage of 48 tells you that with a one-pound pull you should be able to lift a 48-pound load. However, actually your one-pound pull might only lift a 20-pound load. The rest of your effort would be used in overcoming the friction.

www.ingramcontent.com/pod-product-compliance
Lightning Source LLC
Chambersburg PA
CBHW082207300426
44117CB00016B/2700